MW00620670

"As I read this book, it felt like I
inside my mind, heart, and so
book; believe me, the insights
change the trajectory of your l
—Jim Burns, PhD, presi.

with *Your Adult Children: Keep Your Mouth Shut
and the Welcome Mat Out*

"Being close to your grandchild is much more than living down the
street from them. At the core, it's being relationally close no matter
where you live. As Larry Fowler has written in *Overcoming Grandparenting Barriers*, we take a step of faith and extend grace, hope, and
forgiveness in our grandparenting role. And where might we access
those heavenly virtues? As Larry notes, through the grace, hope, and
forgiveness of our Lord. Larry's new book will be an encouragement
as you seek to live out one of your most important roles as a spiritually attuned, proactive grandparent."

—Ken Canfield, PhD, founder of GrandKids Matter

"Grandparenting is a special blessing in life . . . but can also be a
blessed pain! If God created the first family, and they experienced
problems, then I guess we are no exception. Larry Fowler addresses
biblically, vulnerably, and with clarity some of the issues, principles,
and strategies for extended families like ours. I encourage you to read,
weep, pray, persevere, and grow in your wisdom as you lead the way!"

—John Coulombe, interGen Pastor of EvFree Church, Fullerton, CA;
Legacy Coalition founding board member
and director of development

"This book is a godsend for any grandparent who is struggling connecting with their grandchildren due to relationship issues. If your
adult child has walked away from the Lord, perhaps you've been de-
nied the opportunity to give testimony to your grandkids. This book
gives you hope."

—Linda Ranson Jacobs, ambassador of Church Initiative, Inc.

"This book gives hope and much-needed biblical wisdom as well as
practical tools for grandparents in less than ideal relationships with
their children. The insights and applications for rebuilding relationships with grace are so helpful. Larry and Josh have teamed up to

provide biblical wisdom and practical applications that will be used of God to rebuild broken bridges. No doubt this will provide many grandparents with the tools they need to make an eternal impact on their grandchildren and generations to follow."

—George Posthumus, teaching pastor at Riverpark Bible Church, Fresno, CA

"Deeply rooted in God's Word and offering practical insights and suggestions, *Overcoming Grandparenting Barriers* is a must-read for every grandparent, pastor, and Christian counselor!"

—Shawn Thornton, senior pastor of Calvary Community Church, Westlake Village, CA

"I've seen it so often—messy family relationships that leave grandparents discouraged, distressed, hurting, and often hopeless. There has been very little written to address this huge need, so I was very excited to read *Overcoming Grandparenting Barriers*. My friend Larry Fowler's personal stories, his use of Scripture, and his many practical helps create one 'aha' moment after another. I'll be telling every grandparent I know that there is hope!"

—Ron Hunter Jr., PhD, cofounder and director of the D6 Conference and author of *DNA of D6: Building Blocks of Generational Discipleship*

"In his new book, *Overcoming Grandparenting Barriers*, Larry Fowler offers hope, strategies, and new ideas to those who feel 'stuck' in navigating the challenging realities of family dynamics. Drawing on keen insights from the Scriptures, Larry will equip you to trust God's heart, timing, and life-changing power to transform your broken past into His promised future. Larry not only asks the hard questions mined from his personal experience and years of counseling, he offers inspiring perspectives and practical steps that will unleash the gospel of grace in your family! Grandparents, you are a critical tool for spiritual influence and healing, and this book is an answer to your prayers to prepare you for that role."

—Bill Parkinson, cofounding pastor and SageWorks Pastor, Fellowship Bible Church, Little Rock, AR

OVERCOMING
Grandparenting
BARRIERS

OVERCOMING
Grandparenting
BARRIERS

How to Navigate Painful Problems with Grace
and Truth

LARRY FOWLER

DR. JOSH MULVIHILL, GEN. ED.

BETHANYHOUSE
a division of Baker Publishing Group
Minneapolis, Minnesota

Published by Bethany House Publishers
11400 Hampshire Avenue South
Bloomington, Minnesota 55438
www.bethanyhouse.com

Bethany House Publishers is a division of
Baker Publishing Group, Grand Rapids, Michigan

Printed in the United States of America

ISBN 978-0-7642-3132-2

Cover design by Dan Pitts

Author is represented by William Denzel.

19 20 21 22 23 24 25   7 6 5 4 3 2 1

CONTENTS

Series Preface   9

Introduction   11

1. Grandparenting Can Hurt!   15

2. Can't I Just Walk Away from the Pain?   27

3. But They Won't Let Me . . .   39

4. Lord, Where Is the Miracle?   51

5. The Influence Principle   69

6. The Grace Strategy   81

7. Give Me Some Practical Ideas!   93

Notes   103

SERIES PREFACE

GRANDPARENTING MATTERS is a series of short books that address common grandparenting problems with biblical solutions and practical ideas. I have the joy of talking with grandparents all over the country about their God-designed role in the lives of children and grandchildren. Regularly, questions arise about how to do what the Bible says in the midst of barriers, problems, and challenges.

Grandparenting is filled with many joys, but it can also be filled with unexpected pain and problems. Relational tensions, grandparenting restrictions, adult prodigals, grandparents as parents, divorce, long-distance relationships, and blended families all can cause the heart to ache. When brokenness touches our family, we naturally ask questions about how to navigate the challenges.

There are a growing number of resources for Christian grandparents that address the purpose of grandparenting, but few deal with the problem-solving side of family life. We created this series because problems are common, hope is needed, and God's Word provides guidance that can be applied to our unique situations. This series aims to simultaneously comfort and encourage, to equip and edify, as well as to point the way ahead. If you are discouraged or hurting, then I trust you will be blessed by this series.

If you are looking for biblical solutions and practical how-to's, you will find them in these pages.

We've titled the series GRANDPARENTING MATTERS because we believe the Bible teaches that the grandparent-grandchild relationship is important and worthy of our time and attention. Grandparents have a significant impact on the spiritual lives of grandchildren that is second only to parents. Our prayer is that the Gospel is proclaimed, God is honored, your family experiences healing and health, and your children and children's children know, love, and serve Jesus.

Larry Fowler has written a practical book that offers hope and help for the hurting grandparent. As you read this book, remember that hope is found in Christ alone and that help comes from the sufficient Word of God. True transformation is the work of God and is the result of the power of the Gospel. God calls us to be the aroma of Christ and agents of the Gospel to our family. Larry will help you do that in a way that embodies the grace and truth of the Gospel.

If the plain truth of the Gospel does not penetrate the heart, no amount of salesmanship or exemplary living will change the heart of a wayward person. God has given us prayer, told us to seek forgiveness, and called us to Christlike living so that the Gospel can restore and transform your family.

I'm delighted by the high caliber of authors in this series and the impact these books will have on families for their good and for the glory of God. It has been a tremendous privilege to be partners in God's grace with these fine authors. I trust you will be blessed by their godly wisdom, gain a renewed hope in God, experience joy in Christ despite trying circumstances, and be better equipped to be a disciple-making grandparent who passes on a heritage of faith to future generations.

Josh Mulvihill, PhD
Founding Member, the Legacy Coalition
Executive Director of Church and Family Ministry, Renewanation
Connect with me at GospelShapedFamily.com.

INTRODUCTION

Joy.

It's not often that grandparents spend their birthday in a maternity ward, but I did. In fact, I received the best birthday present I've ever been given there: my daughter Andrea gave birth to Tyler, my first grandchild, on the very day of my forty-third birthday. While I don't remember all the details, I do remember my cheeks aching that night from smiling all day long!

Micah, our last-born grandchild and now just two, comes charging through the front door when he visits, finds me, jumps into my arms, and gives me the biggest bear hug his little arms can produce.

From Tyler, our first, to Micah, our last, each grandchild fills our life with joy. I think when you look up "joy" in the dictionary, grandkids ought to be definition number one. Don't you agree? We've all chuckled at the well-worn line, "If I'd known grandkids were this much fun, I would have had them first." We laugh, of course, because it is true: Grandmas get the joy of the newborn without the journey of the pregnancy. Grandpas (usually) get to just report the smell without having to actually change the diaper. Yes, grandparenting usually means you get to enjoy the hugs without the hassles.

Besides bringing joy, the arrival of a grandchild can also bring new hope, even when the circumstances aren't ideal. In one family, new grandmother Teresa was hopeful that through the birth of her granddaughter (the result of a one-night fling), her daughter Megan would become more serious and settle down. In another family, John and Yvonne hoped that with the birth of their grandson, their son and daughter-in-law might take their marriage more seriously and repair the hurts. In still another, Vic prayed that his son would settle into his job and step up to his new responsibility as a father.

But sometimes in the months and years that follow the birth of a grandchild, that joy is crushed, and hope is dashed. When relationships crumble or harsh words leave deep wounds, joy gets pushed aside by anger, bitterness, and resentment. When adult children make bad decisions and bring consequences that affect the whole family, hope fades, and a resignation to a less-than-ideal reality sets in. Let's face it: Being a grandparent can bring the greatest joy life has to offer, but it can also be the conduit of deep pain.

Sometimes the grandparents cause the pain—too much control, too strong opinions, bitterness, bringing up past failures, pride . . . we can be guilty of any or all of those things.

The deeper the relationship, the greater the joy—or the pain—it can bring.

Sometimes the grandparents bear the pain, but the source of it is someone else in the family. A wrong decision by a wayward son can bring excruciating hurt. The divorce of an adult child, with all the accompanying messiness, usually has years of painful consequences. The relational pain and all that accompanies it—worry, bitterness, grief—can devastate. It can cause illness, depression, and thoughts of suicide. It can result in sleepless night after sleepless night. It can suck all the meaning and purpose out of the latter half of life.

I've learned that grandparents have different ways of dealing with their pain. Some grandparents cope by avoiding—walking away from the relationships, away from the hurt. That can lessen the pain, but it also diminishes the possibility for recapturing the joy. Others try to fix it themselves and overreach, causing even more tensions, more hurt, and less chance for resolution. Still others exacerbate the situation by retaliating. Then there are those who respond with wisdom, patience, and love, and God uses them, even through their pain, to be a blessing to their family and a resolution to the situation.

My intent in writing this book is to connect you with the principles of Scripture. Therein lies the greatest hope!

Many, however, just don't know what to do. They've lost hope, feel helpless, and are completely out of ideas. They're stuck. They need hope renewed; they need a new strategy and a bunch of new ideas.

That is the intent of this book: to provide hope, strategies, and new ideas. Much of what you will read is based upon the conversations I've had with grandparents through my ministry as the leader of the Legacy Coalition. Other stories are based upon my own experiences—both successful and not—and those of my family and friends. I've changed many of the names and circumstances in order to protect the privacy of those who have shared with me. In some cases, I simply don't remember who I talked to (though I remember the story), and hence, I've created an illustration based on that conversation. However, every single story, whether actual or fictitious—or partly so—reflects a reality in the world of grandparenting. Many of the stories that have been related to me are heartbreaking, and I have felt so inadequate to give a wise answer and offer a helpful solution.

However, my main source of wisdom is the Bible. I'm a firm believer in the truth and the practicality of Scripture. My whole life is a testimony to that fact; I have never found the advice of God's Word to lead me astray, never found what is presented as truth to be found false. Therefore, my intent in writing this book is to connect you with the principles of Scripture, and by doing so, lead you to a new hope for the situation that is causing you so much pain.

This book will give you *hope*—no matter what your situation is. If you are one of those grandparents who feels hopeless, helpless, and out of ideas—no matter the cause—this book will lift your spirits and restore your resolve. But it will do more than that: As you read, you will also discover *help* in the form of new insights, new direction, and new strategies. Finally, you will find practical tools—*ideas*—that can revitalize your efforts to bring healing and restoration to your family.

Are you ready for a fruitful journey? *Read on.*

1

Grandparenting Can Hurt!

"Mom and Dad, can Andy and I come over and talk with you?"

Dennis and Audrey knew that such a request was unusual from their daughter Megan. After all, they saw her several times a week, and her three kids—their grandkids—as well. It could only mean something serious.

When Andy and Megan came over, they sent the kids into the family room to watch TV, and sat with Dennis and Audrey at the kitchen table.

"Mom, Dad . . ." Megan started. She paused and took a breath. "We have some big news—we've decided to move to Australia."

The news took Audrey's breath away. "Why?" was all she could blurt out. *Australia?* Why so far? Their family was so close, and she loved-*loved*-LOVED seeing her "three little Ds," as she called them (the grandkids were two-year-old Dylan, four-year-old Dacey, and seven-year-old David). How often would she and Dennis see them now? Once a year? Once every five years?

Andy explained. "I've gotten a really good job offer there that would give me a good pay raise, and the cost of living is cheaper."

Megan added, "I know this is a shock to you, Mom and Dad, but I've always lived here. I'd kind of like an adventure—to experience living somewhere else." Dennis and Audrey couldn't remember much of the rest of what was said—they were too numb from the news.

That conversation shook Dennis and Audrey's world. They tried to make the most of every day before the move, seeing the grandkids as much as they could. Then the day of the move came and went, and the loneliness—the *quietness*—set in. Oh, how Audrey missed the hugs and the messes and even their little voices screaming. She could tell Dennis was affected too. He was quieter and seemed to have lost energy.

Christmas that year was the hardest. It was the first time in over thirty years that they celebrated alone—just the two of them. There had been little incentive to decorate; they even discussed not setting up the tree this year, but they decided to do it anyway. It was hard to put their hearts into it. When Christmas Day came, they connected by FaceTime with their "three little Ds," but it was just so quiet, so *different*.

Dennis and Audrey's church held a grandparenting seminar. They went—very reluctantly—because the topic of grandparenting, for them, had morphed from one of delight to one of pain. Their question was, "How can we possibly be an influence in our grandkids' lives when they live so far away?"

They needed *hope* that they could still be involved with their grandkids. They needed *help* in strategizing. In addition, they needed *ideas* of what to do.

Geographical distance is the most common barrier to impacting grandchildren spiritually.

When our organization, the Legacy Coalition, talks about our vision to be intentional Christian grandparents, we are very aware that geographical distance is the most common barrier to impacting grandchildren spiritually—whether that distance is across the Pacific or just across the state.

Dealing with distance has been made much easier by the video capabilities of our smartphones and tablets, but we know those don't quite replace being with them physically. The dilemma of distance increases as grandchildren grow older: Connecting with young grandkids is much easier than staying connected with teenage or young adult grandkids.

Grandparenting from a distance is especially pervasive in Western culture. Our informal surveys in Legacy Coalition seminars and conferences show us that likely over half of American grandparents have at least one grandchild who lives "far away." If geographical distance from grandkids is an issue of yours, you will find some ideas to help bridge the gap in the following pages, but for a whole bookful, I recommend that you get *Long-Distance Grandparenting* by Wayne Rice, another resource in this GRANDPARENTING MATTERS series.

Geographical distance may be the most common obstacle to intentional grandparenting, but it is not the most agonizing. Relational distance is worse, and that is what we address next.

The agony of alienation

Caren and Tom used to take care of Brandon, the youngest of their four grandchildren, three times a week. Either their son David or their daughter-in-law Staci would drop him off early in the morning on their way to work. Caren would get him ready for school, take him there, and pick him up afterward. By that time, Tom would be home from work, and he loved helping Brandon with homework, playing a game together, or tossing a baseball back and forth.

"Tom, have you noticed a change in Staci?" Caren asked her husband one day. "She used to bring Brandon to the door, but I just realized it has been quite a while since she's done that. Lately she just parks in the street and lets him out. She hasn't actually come *in* our house in weeks."

They wondered if—*feared that*—something was wrong. When Tom asked their son, David just said, "Dad, stay out of it." Tom hadn't meant to pry, but David's abrupt pushback left him more convinced that there was a problem. From that conversation forward, their relationship with David was strained as well.

Several days later, Caren got a text from Staci: "We're not going to have you care for Brandon anymore—we're going to put him in the daycare program at school."

Caren was stunned. She didn't text back right away because the whole gamut of emotions swept over her: anger, hurt, fear.

"Why? Haven't we done a good job?" Caren finally texted back.

"We just want him to have the preschool experience," Staci responded. Caren could tell it wasn't the whole story, but she couldn't get Staci to explain further. *Why would Staci do this?* she agonized. Was David in agreement? What had she and Tom done wrong? They *loved* Brandon and took great care of him.

That text from Staci was the first crack in the relationship between Brandon's parents and grandparents. As time went by, Caren and Tom began to see signs that David and Staci's marriage was in trouble, and they surmised that was the reason for Staci's actions. Their fears were confirmed, and a year later Staci and David divorced. They shared custody of Brandon, but that meant Caren and Tom rarely got to see him. When Staci had him, she wouldn't allow it. When David had him, he was afraid of upsetting Staci, so he would let them see Brandon only briefly.

Caren and Tom never fully learned what they did to upset Staci—if anything; communication with her was completely shut off. In fact, Caren said that was the hardest part—not understanding why they weren't allowed to see the grandkids. They could only assume that the issues between Staci and David caused it, and that she took her anger out on them as well as on their son. They had given up trying to connect with her themselves and were praying that David would stand up to her and let them see their grandson. Any mention of the idea, however, only built a taller barrier between them and David, and he would push them further away.

The pain was suffocating, especially to Caren. She told of seeing a Facebook post of the other grandma, Staci's mom, playing with Brandon. She said jealousy and hurt flooded over her, and the anger came back every time she remembered the post. She even took down the pictures of Brandon in their family room because she'd burst into tears nearly every time she looked at them.

Caren and Tom, because of their son's divorce, had been alienated from their grandson. They needed *hope in Christ*—they had lost it. They needed *help from Scripture* in discerning what to do next, and they needed a fresh batch of *ideas* for how to move forward.

Estrangement, or relational distance, takes a huge toll on grandparents. Many go through the grieving process of denial, anger, bargaining, depression, and acceptance, just as if there were a death. But since there *isn't* a death, that process often stagnates, and there is no resolution.

This is one of the greatest hurts of life. It is doubly difficult because not only is there a rift between a parent and their child (the grandparent and the parent), but the grandparent also loses one of the greatest joys of life—a relationship with a grandchild. That hurt can be compounded even more when there is spiritual separation as well.

The suffering of spiritual separation

I had just concluded my vision-casting presentation on the importance of grandparenting to a Sunday morning adult class, when a single grandmother stood up, and with a voice strong enough that most in the room could hear, she revealed her heartbreak:

"But what do I do? My son has said I can either see my granddaughter or I can talk to her about God, but I can never do both. He told me the minute I mention God, I will never be allowed to see my granddaughter again."

I learned more of the story later. Gloria was a Christian, and from the beginning of their marriage, she and her husband, Glenn, had been careful to make church—and other spiritual practices—a priority. However, their son Brian began to reject his spiritual heritage in high school, though Gloria and Glenn did everything they could think of to encourage him back. They gave him books to read and urged him to go to Christian concerts and other events. They tried to talk with him, all to no avail. He continued to drift away through his college years.

Gloria said, "I can still hear his words the first time he told us he no longer believed in our God. That's what he called Him—*our* God. And it wasn't just that he didn't believe; he told us he didn't want to talk about it. So, since we didn't know what else to do, we just kept quiet."

When Brian married and then had a child, Gloria and Glenn did all they could to keep the relationship going. They never brought up spiritual things just so they could be with their adorable granddaughter. Then Glenn died in a car crash as a result of a drunken driver, and Brian took it hard. His atheist perspective turned to anger at the idea of God. When Gloria mentioned seeing Glenn again in heaven, he exploded—"If your God is real, why did He let that guy ever get behind the wheel?"

Gloria's world crashed. Not only was she suffering from loneliness with the loss of her life mate, but Brian—who should have been a comfort or at a minimum, shared her grief—instead would lash out regularly at her faith. There was a constant, underlying tension when they were together, and Gloria feared it would greatly affect her granddaughter.

She wondered if she should just give up. She had lost hope that Brian would come back to God. She was terrified of the cultural influences that her granddaughter would face as she grew up without faith. She stopped talking about anything related to her own faith. And she feared she would see none of them in eternity.

Gloria's story is not only real, it is *common*. Many Christian grandparents suffer silently because their adult children have rejected their faith. And like Caren and Tom, Gloria had lost hope. While there was still a relationship (though strained) with Brian, the spiritual gulf between them was a constant grief to her. She was clueless about what to do. Gloria represents another group of grandparents who need hope, help with a strategy, and some new ideas.

*   *   *   *   *

These three stories illustrate the three greatest hurts of grandparenting, and they are all summarized by the word *distance*. While geographical distance is difficult to overcome, relational distance is even more so. For the Christian grandparent, spiritual distance adds heartbreak on top of heartbreak.

Do you identify with one of these situations? Or maybe with two—are you both geographically and relationally distant from your grandkids? Or is your reality both a relational and spiritual chasm? I get it—your grief is understandable.

The pain is usually private

The adult class leader stood up and said something like, "We have a guest speaker this morning. Larry Fowler is going to share with us about grandparenting. But before he does, let's cover the prayer requests we have on our list." He tapped on his computer and the weekly prayer list appeared on the screen. To myself, I predicted what was going to appear, because I had seen it before. And when the prayer list went up, my expectation was fulfilled: There were about twenty-five prayer requests, and *every one of them was about a physical ailment.*

As I shared with the class and they responded, it became apparent that this group of grandparents was no different from others I had experienced: Many of them were experiencing the pain of

21

a broken relationship with an adult child. Others held the deep disappointment of an adult child who had walked away from their faith. Still others grieved when their son's or daughter's divorce cut off access to grandchildren. Few, however, were aware of how common those pains were.

As in this adult class, it is rare that we reveal the hurt we feel to others in a class setting or in some other public way. Sometimes it is because we are afraid that the request will get back to that son or daughter who is the cause of the pain. Or we are just embarrassed and afraid of what people might think. Christians of our generation have been pretty good at hiding hurt, pretending everything is all right. After all, haven't we been told again and again, in subtle and not-so-subtle ways, that "good" parents don't have kids who abandon faith? Haven't we watched as parents whose kids turned out to be missionaries or pastors were honored and praised? Haven't we heard the sermons that underscore the ideal?

Or maybe it just hurts too much. Maybe we don't want to have to explain everything again. Maybe we are afraid of losing control of our emotions, so we don't share. We end up hiding the thing that hurts the most, and instead ask for prayer about things that are less emotional, less risky, and less revealing, like ailments. But keeping it private doesn't help; in fact, it lessens the possibility that we will receive support from our friends, or biblical ideas of what to do.

It is *real* pain

I've already written that I believe it is *one of the greatest* pains.

You've heard it said, "Mama is only as happy as her most unhappy child." We feel right along with our kids, and that doesn't change when they become adults. What *does* change is the ability to do something about it. When our adult children make wrong choices, we can't control them as we did when they were little, or ground them like we did when they were teenagers. We try; we give them advice, but they don't listen—and usually it just drives a greater wedge between us.

Nearly every time I teach a seminar on grandparenting, some grandpa or grandma wants to talk during a break and share their personal heartbreak. Here are just a few examples of the kinds of hurts people confide:

When our kids were young, we held them in our arms. That stopped as they grew older, but we have never stopped holding them in our hearts.

Janice: "What do I do? My three kids who grew up in the church have all converted to Buddhism. They tell me to keep my Christianity to myself."

Pete: "My wife died four years ago. I've remarried, but my son won't accept my new wife. Because he doesn't like her, he doesn't want her around his children. I've told him I wouldn't come by myself, so now he won't let me see the grandkids. How can I fix this?"

Hank: "My daughter cheated on her husband, which ended their marriage. She's now shacked up with the guy who she cheated with. The children, who live with their dad, are just devastated. He doesn't want any reminder of my daughter, so he doesn't let me around their children much. I let my daughter know how disappointed I was in what she did, and she cut off all communication. I've now lost my daughter and my grandkids. How do I restore my relationship with her without supporting her sinful behavior?"

Darcy: "My granddaughter just made club soccer and almost all the games are on Sundays. Her parents (my son and daughter-in-law) have just stopped going to church. Any time I bring it up, they snap at me and say, 'Mom, she's gonna be fine without so much church.' My granddaughter wants me to come see her play. What do I do?"

Marylou: "My grandkids are terrors. My daughter and son-in-law have completely different ideas of discipline than I do—and theirs don't work. The kids just run wild all over the house, and their parents do nothing. I've tried to help them discipline better, but I've just made them angry with me. They get offended at any suggestions I try to make."

Patti: "Our son eloped with a Christian girl, and their marriage was rocky. A few years ago our daughter-in-law became an atheist activist. Their marriage ended but our son's faith has survived—he attends church regularly with the children. But he is reluctant to push the kids to go, knowing his ex might retaliate and start bringing the kids to the atheist conferences she attends. Our son has cautioned us to 'go easy' with teaching the kids the Bible—to not activate her revenge. We take his caution seriously, yet we wish to take advantage of the opportunity to influence while the grandkids live with us."

Each story is unique, but the reality is similar: deep pain for the grandparents, brokenness in relationships, anger and hurt in the adult children, and negative consequences for the grandchildren.

Why are you reading this book?

What is *your* pain? Why did you pick up this book? What is going on with your kids and grandkids, for which you hope to get some advice, some direction, and some solutions? Right now, before you read further, name it:

I want some hope for . . .
I need some help with . . .
I need some ideas about . . .

Hope. Help. Ideas. We all need them. My prayer has been that as you read this book, you will find some of each. Then as you read each page, keep that thing that is causing you pain front and center, and see how God might guide you in dealing with it.

Comfort from Scripture

- Do you feel like you are walking through the "valley of the shadow of death"? Read Psalm 23 again and allow it to speak to your pain.

- Remember that God may have a wonderful purpose for your pain and grief: "Godly sorrow brings repentance that leads to salvation and leaves no regret, but worldly sorrow brings death" (2 Corinthians 7:10).

- Be assured—*God will give you strength to handle this:* "No temptation has overtaken you except what is common to mankind. And God is faithful; he will not let you be tempted beyond what you can bear. But when you are tempted, he will also provide a way out so that you can endure it" (1 Corinthians 10:13).

Questions to ponder

1. When you became a grandparent, what were you hoping the experience would be like?

2. What was your experience with your own grandparents, and how did that impact your expectations for your role as a grandparent?

3. Which one (or more) of the "distances" is part of your experience now with your grandchildren? Geographical, relational, or spiritual?

4. Do you agree with the author that the pains of grandparenting are usually kept private, not usually revealed in church and social settings? Why or why not?

5. How do you react to the statement that the pains of grandparenting are some of the greatest pains of life?

6. What do you hope to get out of this book? Hope, help, or ideas?

2

Can't I Just Walk Away from the Pain?

There are some powerful reasons to redouble your efforts to impact your grandchildren spiritually. If you are experiencing pain in your grandparenting role, the easy way out might be to ignore the problems and just go on with life. If you are tempted to do that, then rethink your response in light of the following:

Reason #1: The Bible's ideal concerning grandparenting

The Bible is filled both with challenges to live up to the ideal and narratives concerning what is real. The most famous ideal of the Old Testament is, of course, the Ten Commandments. In the New Testament, Jesus challenged us with an ideal when He said the greatest commandment was to "Love the Lord your God with all your heart and with all your soul and with all your mind."[1] The apostle Peter gave us another when he wrote, "Be holy in all you do."[2]

On the other hand, examples of what is real—*failures*—are also frequent in the stories of Scripture: Moses' loss of temper,

Abraham's compromise, David's adultery, Thomas's unbelief, Peter's cowardice. The biblical accounts of failure to meet the ideal only illustrate the fallen nature of our world and the people in it.

None of us have followed the Scripture ideals completely either, have we? Every one of us has broken a commandment, loved God less than completely, and been unholy in things we do. Yet our *real* situations shouldn't make us reject the biblical *ideals*; they help us deal with our realities in the wisest way when they remain a target for us in how we respond to daily life.

The Bible also has an ideal for grandparenting. We find God's *intended outcome* of our efforts expressed in verses like these:

> He decreed statutes for Jacob
> and established the law in Israel,
> which he commanded our ancestors to teach their children,
> so the next generation would know them,
> even the children yet to be born,
> and they in turn would tell their children.
>
> Psalm 78:5–6

> Tell it to your children,
> and let your children tell it to their children,
> and their children to the next generation.
>
> Joel 1:3

> So that you, your children and their children after them may fear the Lord your God as long as you live.
>
> Deuteronomy 6:2

In each of these passages, it is clear God intends that our grandparenting results in faith perpetuated through future generations. This truth gives our lives—in particular, the last half of life—significant purpose.

God also has an ideal for our grandparenting *activity*:

28

Only be careful, and watch yourselves closely so that you do not forget the things your eyes have seen or let them fade from your heart as long as you live. Teach them to your children and to their children after them.

Deuteronomy 4:9

God intends that our grandparenting result in faith perpetuated through future generations.

This verse tells us grandparents are to be spiritual teachers, not only of our children, but also of our grandchildren. We are to teach *two* generations! Think about it: If we are able to flesh out this idea, then six believing adults will be influencing each family of children. It looks like this:

GOD'S IDEAL: six adults spiritually influencing each family of children

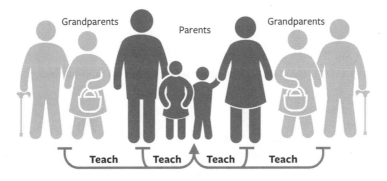

However, our families often don't look like that. Even the Bible has a number of examples where children followed God even though their family situation was less than ideal:

- *Timothy* was a young man of great faith, as were his mother and grandmother. Scripture doesn't mention a father or grandfather. Since they are not mentioned, we might assume they were absent, at least from the perspective of guiding him in his faith (2 Timothy 1:5).

29

- *Asa, fifth king of Israel.* After David, a steady decline in devotion to God began in Solomon, continued in Rehoboam, bottomed in Abijah, and then Asa came to power—a king devoted to God, even though his parents and likely all his grandparents were not (1 Kings 15:9–11).
- *The Old Testament Joseph*, one of the shining examples of godliness, came from a family that was filled with jealousy, feuding, and trouble (Genesis 37:3–4).

You may identify more with one of those "real" stories than you do with the ideal. In fact, your family may be really far from the ideal. In many families, the parents aren't doing their job of spiritual training. In others, the grandkids get bombarded with mixed messages—sometimes from the two sets of grandparents. Maybe there are no other grandparents, or there is no father in the picture. Maybe yours looks something like this, and nobody else teaches the kids about God but you:

WHAT IS REAL: many influencers are either absent or not believers

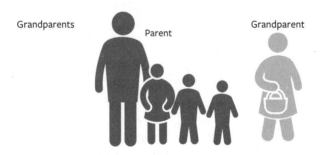

Grandparents   Parent   Grandparent

Even if your family doesn't look at all like an intact nuclear family with two sets of grandparents, *you* must still pursue the ideal, in terms of what you are responsible for. You may be the only grandparent who cares about spiritual things—or even the only adult in your grandchild's life who is a Christ-follower. God still wants you to tell your faith stories, pray, and do all you can to influence future generations for Him! You, however, might need to be creative to find productive ways for that to take place.

In the case of grandparenting, how we respond in real-life situations must be informed by God's ideal. It never changes—reality does, but God's best doesn't. No matter how hopeless, how difficult you think it might be to try to influence grandchildren for God, doing it His way must be your aim, your intent. You will respond differently—*better*—when you keep that in view.

Reason #2: Your incredible potential

Eunice and Lois, Timothy's mother and grandmother, must have had an incredible impact on that boy—so much so that the apostle Paul recognized it years later when Timothy was his companion and fellow missionary. As a grandparent, you also have the potential for that kind of impact.

Remember Caren and Tom? They were so stymied by the divorce of their son and daughter-in-law that they had given up hope of regular contact with their grandson Brandon—to say nothing of spiritual impact. In a private conversation with me, they questioned, "What good does it do to study Scripture about the role of a grandparent when we are never going to have an opportunity to influence?"

"The potential is still there," I told them. "It just isn't being realized now because of the relational barrier you have. I understand that it seems impossible to overcome. But suppose it *wasn't* there—suppose that the relationship could be repaired. Might you then be able to impact Brandon?"

Grandparent, you are potentially an ideal discipler of your grandchildren.

"Of course," Tom responded. "But I don't think things are going to change. We've been praying that David would take him to church when he has him, but that only happens occasionally." Tom wasn't convinced at that point, but he did begin to think differently about his family.

31

Grandparent—you may feel that the opportunity to influence has been lost, just like Caren and Tom did. However, that doesn't mean the *potential* has disappeared, does it? You are in a prime role as grandparent (remember, we're talking potential here) to be a spiritual mentor. Think about the following statements and relate them to the role of grandparent:

> *Spiritual mentors are most effective when they are wise.* Your years of experience—including those times when you failed as well as when you succeeded—qualify you. Don't you agree that you know more now than you did when you were a young parent?

> *Spiritual mentors are at their best when they can love deeply and unconditionally.* Who better than a grandparent to truly love a child? Their other mentors in life—teachers, coaches, etc.—may say they love them, but they will never have the kind of relationship that grandparents do. Other than the parent, *no one* will love that child like you.

> *Spiritual mentors are most effective when they have a deep, long-term relationship with their disciples.* If you are praying that your grandchild might go to church, remember the limitations there: Any children's or youth worker will likely develop a relationship with your grand for less than a year. It will be in a group situation. The number of hours of connection will likely be about twenty to thirty *per year* (the kids just don't attend often enough). There simply isn't the opportunity for those at church to develop a childhood-long relationship like you can. Of course you still want them to go, but the church has limitations, and you are better positioned for long-term influence.

The wisdom you have, the deep love you feel, and the long-term involvement you desire make you—*potentially*—an ideal discipler of your grandchildren. Don't lose sight of that possibility!

Reason #3: You care so much

Who cares more than you do about the spiritual life of your grandchild?

When I was serving as a coach and consultant to children's pastors in large churches in America, I would often encourage them to look at some statistics that were almost always ignored: "I'm not interested in how many children you have in your ministry, I want to know how often they come." When they looked, the lowness of the numbers was surprising—even horrifying. One large church that had 1,243 children in their ministry had only fifty-two of them coming regularly (we defined that as three times a month or more). That percentage was repeated over and over again. Many children's pastors said the average child attended only once a month. Some estimated that they had, on an average, only fifteen hours *per year* to influence their children for God. Parents have been alarmingly inconsistent in bringing their children to church.

But we discovered that two groups attended frequently—two that defied the odds. One was the children of the workers themselves; they were much more regular in attendance. The second group: children who were *brought by grandparents*. Why did that make a difference? I think there is only one reason—grandparents simply care more about a child's spirituality. *That's* why a grandpa or grandma would go by the grandkids' house, often get them dressed, take them to church, and then return them home later.

How about you? Do you now care more—or less—about the spiritual lives of those who follow you in your family than you did when you were a young parent? When I teach seminars and ask that question, nearly all hands go up indicating that they care more as grandparents than they did as parents. In general, parents care more about grades, achievement in athletics, behavior. But grandparents have a different perspective—they see a much bigger picture—a *spiritual* picture.

Reason #4: It gives you the best purpose in this stage of life

A few years ago I was enjoying a trusted and comfortable role as part of the executive leadership team of my ministry, Awana. God began disrupting my comfort as I studied Scripture, and I became convinced that my best efforts in this stage of life should be focused on family. As a result, I took a lesser role in the ministry, and Diane and I moved from Chicago to Southern California for the express purpose of being in a position to influence our grandchildren as they grew and developed. God has been very gracious in giving us the opportunity to be very involved in their lives.

Many grandparents haven't found this purpose. Recently I had lunch with Jarrod, and he shared with me this experience: "When our first child was born, I expected my parents to be excited. When they came to see our newborn, just about the first sentence out of their mouths was, 'Now, don't expect us to baby-sit. Our lives are already full enough.' We got pretty much the same response from my wife's parents. So we have been on our own in raising our kids."

Jarrod's comments were made in the context of a conversation about how he and his wife wanted to be different grandparents than that. But his account of how his parents viewed grandparenting illustrates what we often observe in our generation. Jarrod's parents believed the cultural lie that the later years are to be about enjoying yourselves (your retirement), taking trips, "spending your kids' inheritance," etc. It is what I call "retirement narcissism."

That kind of a life will soon prove empty. The golf scores will stop improving, the cruises will start feeling all the same, and family relationships may suffer even more.

On the other hand, God's plan for grandparents—investing in future generations so that they follow Him—gives great purpose. If we believe in eternity, we see the "fourth quarter" of life as preparatory rather than the last hurrah. What greater purpose could we have than to do all we can to see that our descendants are in eternity with us!

Reason #5: Your grandkids need you!

Grandchildren are healthier emotionally, socially, psychologically, and spiritually when they have a healthy dose of grandparent involvement—unless, of course, the grandparent involvement takes the form of interference with or subversion of the parent's role. Your participation in their lives blesses them in so many ways! And if the barriers you face have hidden this truth from you, consider the following:

Grandparents love differently than parents. Sometimes negative behavior or performance issues can impact the expression of love that children experience from their parents, but grandparent love is not so affected by those things. It is expressed more easily because unless they are the caregivers, grandparents are not responsible for the homework, discipline, hectic schedules, and other pressures that dominate a parent's time.

> **Grandchildren are healthier emotionally, socially, psychologically, and spiritually when they have a healthy dose of grandparent involvement.**

Grandparent involvement gives grandchildren a sense of identity and heritage. Every child needs to belong and know they belong. When there is a strong identity found in an extended family, that child will be less likely to crave it elsewhere. It is a powerful antidote to our young people being overly influenced by their peers during their teenage years and beyond.

Grandparents provide additional, positive adult role models that are vital to a child's worldview. They provide a source of independent-from-parent experiences that are still wrapped in love and safety. These are critical in helping a child move healthily from childhood dependence to adult independence.

Grandpa, Grandma—you are so important to your grandchild! Don't ever underestimate the significance of your role!

Challenges from Scripture

- What is your purpose in this last half of life? How about this: "And even when I am old and gray, O God, do not forsake me, until I declare Your strength to this generation, Your power to all who are to come" (Psalm 71:18 NASB).

- One thing you can do for sure, no matter your situation— watch your own life and testimony: "Only be careful, and watch yourselves closely so that you do not forget the things your eyes have seen or let them fade from your heart as long as you live" (Deuteronomy 4:9).

- Meditate on this verse: "I am reminded of your sincere faith, which first lived in your grandmother Lois and in your mother Eunice and, I am persuaded, now lives in you also" (2 Timothy 1:5). What might Paul have known about Lois and Eunice that would have caused him to commend them?

Questions to ponder

1. When our real situation is less than ideal from a biblical point of view, what should we do? How do you react to the premise that keeping God's ideal in mind helps us be wiser when we deal with our family's reality?

2. Think about your grandchildren. Who cares more than you do about their spiritual growth and development (not counting parents)? How does that impact what you think and do?

3. If someone had asked you before you started reading this book, "What is your purpose in life right now?" how would you have answered? Is your thinking beginning to change one way or another?

4. Is your presence (or non-presence) in your grandchildren's life a positive or a negative for them?

5. If you are in conflict with their parents, or the relationship is broken, what could you begin praying for now that you haven't prayed for before?

3

But They Won't Let Me . . .

When I am teaching a seminar and someone approaches me with a concern during a break between sessions, I can just about guarantee that they will start with a phrase like, "But they [the parents] won't let me . . ." The rest of the sentence could be "see the grandkids," or "say anything about God," or something similar. Sometimes they have tears in their eyes because of the deep hurt, and I empathize with their pain. Those first words out of their mouth, though, reveal wrong thinking—thinking that is focused more on them than it should be. It is as if they want to establish from the beginning that the parents are the problem, not themselves. Often, they may be right—but if they are to make progress in their dilemma, they must learn to think differently.

This is the premise for this chapter: *If you are to find hope for the hurt you are experiencing, you must first examine how you think, and make sure that your mind and heart are aligned with what Scripture says.*

God is always more concerned with our inner person than He is with our outer person; He's concerned more with our heart than with our actions. So hold off for a bit on *doing* something; start instead by making sure you are *thinking* the way God wants you to think.

> Therefore, I urge you, brothers and sisters, in view of God's mercy, to offer your bodies as a living sacrifice, holy and pleasing to God—this is your true and proper worship.
> Do not conform to the pattern of this world, but be transformed by the renewing of your mind. Then you will be able to test and approve what God's will is—his good, pleasing and perfect will.
>
> Romans 12:1–2

As you see in verse one, we are to offer our bodies as a living sacrifice, and the way we do this begins with us renewing our minds (v. 2). In this chapter, we'll seek to describe how you might be able to *renew your grandparent mind* to align with how God desires you to think.

Thinking rightly about others

I want you to do an exercise. Take a sheet of paper and make a list of the adults in your family—you, your spouse, your adult children, and their spouses. When you're done, then come back to reading this book. Okay—if you don't actually write them down, list them mentally.

Finished? Have your list ready? Now—next step—circle the names of the people who *you* can change.

When I did it, there was only one name circled—mine. I can't change my wife, Diane (of course, I wouldn't want to—I think she's perfect). I also can't change my children or their spouses. Only they—and God—can.

Read this as if you are giving advice to yourself: "I can only change myself; I cannot change others."

But we *want* to change others, don't we? And when we try, we are too often left with unintended and even unproductive results.

In fact, it's pretty likely that when you picked up this book, you were hoping for some formula, some technique, or some words of wisdom you could use to change that adult child of yours, or whoever is causing you pain.

You're not going to find it. Why? Because you can't change others.

I can only change myself; I cannot change others.

Look at what Scripture says: "Only be careful, and watch yourselves closely so that you do not forget the things your eyes have seen or let them fade from your heart as long as you live. Teach them to your children and to their children after them" (Deuteronomy 4:9).

Notice who we are to watch: *ourselves*. In this command to pass on our faith to future generations, we are to keep our eyes on us. It's so easy to want to change others, but leave that to God, and watch yourself.

Denise and James *wanted* their son Darin to change so badly. He had started running with the wrong crowd after high school, had dabbled in drugs, and had been arrested numerous times for drunken driving, disorderly conduct, and more. Darin had moved in with a girlfriend a few miles away, which upset his parents further. He would come around to see them occasionally, and if they brought up his lifestyle, he would shut them down: "If you're going to bring that up, I'm leaving." If they continued to press the issue, Darin did just what he said he would do—leave. They wouldn't see him again for quite a while—something they felt he was doing to punish them. James told me, "Somebody has got to talk some sense into that kid—and if we don't, who will?" But it seemed every attempt to talk to him made the barrier between them even higher. "What we're doing isn't working, and we don't know what else to try."

Denise and James's efforts to change Darin were proving to be counterproductive. The more they tried to give him advice, the more he pulled away. The harder they worked to convince him he was doing wrong, the more he seemed drawn to it. They needed a new strategy, a new approach.

And that new approach was this: Denise and James needed to focus on how *they* could change.

You see, for those of us who have adult children like Darin, if *we* change, we might be more effective in helping *them* change. It may be that our unwillingness to change our approach is a barrier to that son-in-law changing. It might also be that if *we* change, that might just be the thing God uses to bring about a transformation in that daughter-in-law.

The rest of this book is all about *you* changing. Changing how you think, changing your strategy, changing how you respond. Then, as you change, God may give you the privilege of being an instrument in His hands as He changes others in your family.

Will you pray this prayer?

God, please forgive me for being more focused on changing others than on how I need to change myself. I want to change my perspective; help me to learn better behaviors and have more Christlike attitudes.

Change me first, Lord.

Thinking rightly about time

God never lets pain go to waste. However, we often can't see a big enough picture to know how He ends up using it for His purposes.

When our littlest grandson, Micah (age two), stays with us, he often gets hungry about 4:30 or 5:00. He'll go to the pantry and say, "Gamma, I have a 'nola bar?" When Diane says, "No, Micah, it's almost time for supper," he doesn't get it: A half-hour or an hour wait until supper doesn't compute. He wants his hunger pang fixed *now*! But his grandma has a bigger picture than he does. His sense of time is only for the moment; hers is much longer.

There's a big difference between Micah's perceptions of time and Diane's. There's an even wider chasm between our understanding of time and God's. We may be mature enough to have a decades-long perspective, but God's perspective is even beyond measuring by millennia—it is, of course, infinite.

Here's the problem: We often see pain through the lens of our own experience, our own situation, our own family, our own time frame—instead of attempting to see the bigger picture that God sees.

Remember the story of Moses? I have thought of the mother of the Egyptian that he killed in anger way back in the book of Exodus. We don't know anything about her, of course, and she's not mentioned in Scripture—but we can surmise some things about her.

First, like any mother, she loved her son. Second, she likely knew of his job of being the slave master over some Israelites. Third, she deeply grieved when she learned that her son had been murdered. Fourth, she had no way to see God's plan for using that experience in Moses' life. Yet He used that awful incident to carry out His plan for His people.

How? God used that life-disrupting experience in Moses' life to drive him into the wilderness. Likely, he would have never gone had something like that not happened.

God then used the forty years in the wilderness to get Moses ready to lead the children of Israel. By the time Moses returned to Egypt, that mother probably had died. She never saw that the murder of her son—such an awful, awful thing—was a circumstance that God used for good—for the deliverance of His people.

Think about the people the apostle Paul persecuted before he became a believer; their pain was incredible as well. Yet God no doubt used their pain to impact Paul after Christ encountered him. The transformation from persecutor to preacher, which was such a powerful testimony to Paul's listeners, would not have been possible without those who had been persecuted.

Is it possible that God will use the hurt you are experiencing in your family in some way you will never see? Might it be used to accomplish a purpose in someone who is not even part of your family? Might He use the hurt for His glory in the life of a grandchild? Or someone not even yet born? Might He use the pain to accomplish His purposes in several people's lives—in different ways?

God may use our hurts in a time that we will never see, in a person we will never know, or in a place we will never visit.

"Yes, it's possible," you might say, "but that doesn't alleviate the pain I'm feeling right now." Of course it doesn't. But if you are going to deal with your hurt, you need to trust that God has a bigger picture in mind.

You know of the promise of Romans 8:28, don't you?

> And we know that in all things God works for the good of those who love him, who have been called according to his purpose.

Can I remind you that the verse doesn't say, "in all things God works for *my* good"? It may be someone else's good that God has in mind in allowing this difficult circumstance.

He may use our hurts in a time we will never see, in a person we will never know, or in a place we will never visit. We must trust Him. We must trust His goodness. We must trust His perspective that is far beyond ours—just like grandma Diane's perspective is far beyond two-year-old Micah's.

Will you pray this prayer?

> *God, I am going to trust your perspective. I understand you see a bigger picture than I do, so I trust your wisdom to use this for good, whether I see it or not. I entrust time—and timing—to you.*
>
> *I trust you, Lord.*

Thinking rightly about the problem

You know that thing that upsets you so much? Your son's wrong decisions, your daughter's divorce, the broken communication and the lack of spiritual interest on the part of your teenage grandkids . . . ? I have a question to ask you: Are you shouldering that burden yourself? How would God have you think about it?

Jennifer shared that she had been struggling to sleep well. Her thoughts late at night often turned to her two adult sons, who regularly disappointed her with wrong decisions. For example, one had bought an unneeded, customized pickup truck on a whim, without asking his wife first—and it put his young family in a huge financial pinch. Jennifer wondered if she should confront him, bail him out, or just wait. But that was just one example; each immature decision her sons made brought a new series of sleepless nights. "They're my *sons*—I just care so much about them. What can I do?" she asked.

I asked Jennifer if she would classify her middle-of-the-night thoughts as worry.

"Yes, I guess I am a worrier," she replied.

"Do you, as their mother, feel some responsibility to fix the messes that your sons keep getting in?" I asked.

Jennifer confessed, "I do."

"Jennifer, I think that while you profess to be a child of God, you're not living in His kingdom—you're still stuck in this world's kingdom." She looked puzzled. "The reason I know is because *I do the same thing—and I do it way too often.* When I have stress and anxiety, I lay awake wondering how *I* am going to fix the problem, and *I* feel the load on my shoulders.

We care *about* the problem, but we let God carry the problem.

"We both need to remember to live in His kingdom, not in this world. That means that while we care, our care doesn't become worrying. We *care* about the problem, but we don't *carry* the problem—we let God do that."

Instead of her worrying, I challenged her to do three things:

1. Pray that God's power be displayed through the issue.
2. Give the responsibility she feels to fix things over to Him.
3. Trust that He will fix it in His way, in His time.

Which kingdom are you in? Can you rise above this messed-up, broken world, with all of its hurts and disappointments, and live in God's kingdom? If you're a child of God, you have citizenship there—so see your problems from that perspective.

Which column represents the way you think about the problem you are facing?

THE VIEW: *from God's kingdom*	THE VIEW: *from this messed-up, broken world*
"God, I know you care even more than I do."	"I am so concerned about this."
"Will you carry this, Lord?"	"I just don't know what I'm going to do."
"I know you will use this for good, even if I can't see it."	"I am so scared of how this is going to end."
"I give the responsibility for this over to you."	"I've got to find a way to fix it."
"I thank you for the victory that you will win in this."	"This is going to end in a disaster."

The apostle Paul describes how we are to think in this passage (notice that there is no room for worry in this list):

Finally, brothers and sisters, whatever is true, whatever is noble, whatever is right, whatever is pure, whatever is lovely, whatever is admirable—if anything is excellent or praiseworthy—think about such things.

Philippians 4:8

When we think rightly, the next step is to do right:

> Whatever you have learned or received or heard from me, or seen in me—put it into practice.
>
> Philippians 4:9

When we think rightly and do right, look at what the result is, according to the last part of the verse: "And the God of peace will be with you" (Philippians 4:9).

Is the way you are looking at the problem producing peace—or worry? Ask God to help you think correctly about the issues you are facing today.

Will you pray this prayer?

God, I give my worrying over to you. Since I have done all I can to fix the situation that concerns me, I now give it over to you. I know you are going to use it for good, whether I see that or not.

I trust you, Lord.

Thinking rightly about the past

We all have things in our past that have happened with our kids, our grandkids, or with ourselves that we'd give anything to go back and change. Unfortunately, we can't.

Maybe you'd like to change who your daughter married. You'd love to go back and insert *your* choice for her husband, instead of the loser *she* chose. If this describes your feelings, you need to tell yourself that you just can't do it. That son-in-law is the one you have, and you need to accept it.

Maybe you'd like to take back the angry words you said in a big fight that contributed to a huge rift between your son and yourself. You'd like to un-say them, but you can't. No matter how many times we ask God to forgive us, we can't shake the regret. If that's you, recognize that those words are out of your mouth and there's no way you can stuff them back in. Think instead about what you can do from this point forward.

Maybe you would like to go back and have not allowed your teenager to attend that weekend party, when the binge drinking started. But now that teenager is a young adult and has alcohol dependency. Oh, how you wish you had stood your ground more firmly. You feel partly responsible for her downward spiral, and the regret still causes sleepless nights.

Wouldn't it be amazing if we could go back and undo things? Change the past?

But you know the truth; in fact, you've heard it hundreds of times and have said it yourself: You *can't* change the past. So let go of the regrets. Stop thinking *If only* . . . It does absolutely no good.

You and I can only change the future. Start now, and see what you can do to impact the days and months and years ahead of you.

Will you pray this prayer?

God, please forgive me for dwelling on the past. I know I can't change it. Help me to start fresh, looking forward to how I can change in the future.

I put the future in your hands, and want to be an instrument for change.

I trust you, Lord.

Seeing my world the way God would have me see it—oh, that is so tough. Yet hope for a different future isn't found in wallowing in the attitudes of the past. It is found in a new perspective—a better perspective. Here are the three aspects of this new perspective that you must embrace:

I can only change myself; I cannot change others.

I must give to God what I cannot fix myself.

I can't change the past; I can only impact the future.

Do you want help? Hope? It starts with seeing both from God's perspective rather than your own.

Insight from Scripture

- The prophet Habakkuk voiced his frustration at the beginning of the book bearing his name: "How long, Lord, must I call for help, but you do not listen? Or cry out to you, 'Violence!' but you do not save? Why do you make me look at injustice? Why do you tolerate wrongdoing? Destruction and violence are before me; there is strife, and conflict abounds. Therefore the law is paralyzed, and justice never prevails. The wicked hem in the righteous, so that justice is perverted" (Habakkuk 1:2–4).

- At the end of the book, this is his perspective: "Though the fig tree does not bud and there are no grapes on the vines, though the olive crop fails and the fields produce no food, though there are no sheep in the pen and no cattle in the stalls, yet I will rejoice in the Lord, I will be joyful in God my Savior" (Habakkuk 3:17–18).

- Can you share his patience and his trust in God?

- How does this verse impact your perspective of time and how quickly God might deal with the situation that so concerns you? "But you, Lord, are a compassionate and gracious God, slow to anger, abounding in love and faithfulness" (Psalm 86:15).

Questions to ponder

1. Do you really believe that you cannot change others? Think through your family members; which ones have you tried to change? What has been the result?

2. Why is trying to change someone else often counterproductive? Can you think of an illustration?

3. How is confronting destructive or sinful behavior (which is certainly appropriate in some situations) different from "trying to change someone"?

3. Do you have the kind of faith that will trust God to use your hurt to accomplish His purposes in a way you might never see?

4. Can you think of an instance where God used one person's hurt to accomplish something significant in someone else's life?

5. Are you a worrier? Or are you able to give your problems over to God and trust Him to carry them? Can you practice the "care, but don't carry" principle in regard to the things that concern you?

4

Lord, Where Is the Miracle?

God, why can't you just perform a miracle? Do you ever think that? *If you really have power, why don't you answer my prayer and do something?*

Job's despair

The Old Testament patriarch Job had reached that depth of frustration. You're likely familiar with the overwhelming trials he endured at the beginning of the book bearing his name, but those weren't the total of his woes; things continued to spiral downward.

As his friends verbally chastised him, he felt no one was listening. He felt completely powerless and cried out for help: "If only there were someone to mediate between us . . ." (9:33). Then, the all-time low for him is in chapter 19, when—after his friends had accused him of bad motives, secret sins, pride, and everything else they could think of—he felt there was no place to turn. His description of his situation is incredibly bleak:

My relatives have gone away;
  my closest friends have forgotten me. . . .
My breath is offensive to my wife;
  I am loathsome to my own family.
Even the little boys scorn me . . .
All my intimate friends detest me . . .
I am nothing but skin and bones . . .
  the hand of God has struck me.

Job 19:14, 17–21

Job needed help. More than that even, he needed hope. But help from God didn't come—and hope vanished. He was beyond desperate:

"I cry out to you, God, but you do not answer; I stand up, but you merely look at me. . . . Surely no one lays a hand on a broken man when he cries for help in his distress. . . . Yet when I hoped for good, evil came; when I looked for light, then came darkness."

Job 30:20, 24, 26

Where IS God when we need Him?

We may not verbalize our despair like Job did, but we very well think it. Like Job, we feel helpless—even *hopeless*—in our situation, and wish God would intervene. We think we've been pretty loyal followers, and He really ought to respond to our cries for help. Yet—He doesn't; at least not on our timetable or according to our plan. Here's the way the "Job dilemma" plays out in grandparenting today:

- Jenni wished her daughter's divorce and all the accompanying nightmarish consequences would just go away. She felt like the drama would never end! Why didn't God intervene and heal the marriage like she had prayed?
- Ted's son Kevin kept going back to his addictions. Despite repeated promises that he would stay clean, Kevin wasn't

shaking his habits. It was bankrupting the family, traumatizing his children (Ted's grandkids), and had already ruined his marriage. Where was God's power when Kevin had prayed and asked for deliverance from his troubles?

• Dennis and Keri had been great parents, but daughter Amanda was a "wild child" who relished doing the exact opposite of what she had been taught as a child. Her in-their-face defiance of God and all they had tried to teach her broke their hearts. When they tried to remind her of God's displeasure with her lifestyle, she'd laugh at them, belittle their beliefs, and threaten to cut off all communication with her and her children if they continued to bring it up. Dennis and Keri were scared to death about the impact her unbridled lifestyle would have on their precious grandkids. Every attempt they made to intervene seemed to only make matters worse. They were losing hope.

Each one of these shared Job's position—one of lost hope, helplessness, and despair. They wanted to fix the pain in their family but felt completely powerless to do so. They wondered why their prayers were going unanswered.

When I was nineteen, I worked as a counselor at a Christian camp during the summer. I was already a sincere Christ-follower and felt called to ministry. I recall being really motivated to learn how to experience the power of God. More specifically, I became obsessed with wanting to find out a "secret" to seeing God demonstrate His power through me. I talked with the camp pastor, read books that were recommended to me, and discussed it with everyone I could think of. After a while, the curiosity faded, and in looking back, I realized that I never really discovered a definitive answer to my quest at that time.

Now I'm much older. I've studied Scripture, and I've learned some secrets to the power of God. I've seen the display of God's power in my life and in my family. I've seen family members and friends amazingly transformed as they responded to the Gospel or submitted to Christ's lordship. I've seen God miraculously orchestrate circumstances to accomplish amazing things. I've learned He *does* provide, and He *does* work.

I have also learned that it is always in His time and done His way.

I want to share with you four secrets to God's power straight from Scripture. The first has to do with a mindset; the second, with a message; and the third and fourth, with action.

Secret #1: Delighting in weakness

Weakness—this is the *mindset* that is an avenue for spiritual power. You may not recognize it, but if you feel weak, at a loss for what to do, you may be exactly where God wants you. When we feel we have nowhere to turn and that hope has evaporated, then we are in the position where God can do His greatest work in us.

Here's why: We learn the most about ourselves—and God—when life is hard, not when it is easy. Think back over your life. When have you grown the most spiritually? When life's waters were calm, with a soft, gentle breeze, or when you were

We learn the most about God when life is hard, not when it is easy.

facing a hurricane? For me, it's been the hurricane. I imagine it has been the same for you.

In fact, I believe that people whose lives have been one of sailing on calm waters do not know some things about God that I have learned. Calm waters don't teach us to rely on God; hurricanes do. We don't need God (we think) when we have gentle breezes blowing; but let us experience the force of hurricane winds, and we are driven into a position to depend on God.

Look what the prophet Isaiah said: "He gives strength to the weary and increases the power of the weak" (Isaiah 40:29). Notice to whom God gives strength—the weary and the weak. I've certainly found that to be true. Here's when I have experienced the power of God the most, and grown the most:

- *When I had a serious, long-term debilitating illness.* I suffered with chronic fatigue syndrome for seventeen years. During the early days of that disease, when the intense nerve pain and fatigue was so debilitating, God did some major surgery on my young-man's ego and my pride. I would never have learned to submit to God in the way I have without going through those very difficult days.

- *When money was so tight* we didn't know if we had enough to buy food for the week. During those times, I was more grateful for every dollar, more careful to pray for God's provision. When our finances have been comfortable, I have been slower to be thankful, slower to pray.

- *When there was a family crisis.* Every family has them—we certainly have. Whether it was illness, wrong decisions that we or one of our kids made, or something else, it drove me to pray. It caused me to put God back on the throne of my life and reassess my priorities.

Have you learned the same thing? The apostle Paul had. His testimony in 2 Corinthians 12:7–10 reveals he knew this:

> I was given a thorn in my flesh, a messenger of Satan, to torment me. Three times I pleaded with the Lord to take it away from me. But he said to me, "My grace is sufficient for you, for my power is made perfect in weakness." Therefore I will boast all the more gladly about my weaknesses, so that Christ's power may rest on me. That is why, for Christ's sake, I delight in weaknesses, in insults, in hardships, in persecutions, in difficulties. For when I am weak, then I am strong.

Do you see Paul's list of problems in this passage?

Weaknesses . . . insults . . . hardships . . . persecutions . . . difficulties. We normally plead with God to get us out of those things. "God, deliver (or heal) Joe from _____" is about the most common small-group prayer that is uttered. But Paul's attitude is the exact opposite: He *boasts* about them; he *delights* in them. If Paul were in Joe's small group today, he might pray, "God, thank you for putting Joe into a _____." Why? Because he had learned that when he was weak, Christ's power was on him. He knew the secret: *God's power is made perfect in our weakness.*

Weakness is not simply a physical condition; we can be weak in experience, weak in wisdom, weak emotionally. Each of these provides an opportunity for God's power to be seen more clearly.

Do you understand, Christian grandparent, that if you feel like hope is running out, then you are in an ideal position to see God work? You are perfectly situated to grow spiritually, and the bleakness of your life right now creates an ideal backdrop for an awesome display of God's power.

If it seems like your adult son is never going to come back to God, or that your daughter-in-law will never warm up to you, or your teenage grandson will not stop doing drugs, your family is in a prime location for God to do something amazing. You are in a spot where, when God works, there will be no doubt who supplied the spiritual power.

So, can you adopt Paul's perspective concerning your difficulty? Can you delight in your weakness—because you understand that your situation provides an opportunity for God's great power to be on display?

Can you pray this?

God, I delight in this difficulty.

I am thankful that this is an opportunity for your great power to be displayed. I feel privileged to be in such an opportunity. I can't wait to see how you are going to display your power!

Thank you, Lord!

Secret #2: The Gospel

There is incredible power in the message of the Gospel. It simply transforms lives. You know that already, don't you? I know it.

We know it because we have experienced it ourselves. And we know it because the Bible tells us so: "For the message of the cross is foolishness to those who are perishing, but to us who are being saved it is the power of God" (1 Corinthians 1:18).

Both parts of that truth have played out for two thousand years, haven't they? Unbelievers see the Gospel as foolishness, and in contrast, we who have experienced it know different. Just one of those down through history who knew of the power was Lewis E. Jones, a classmate of early-nineteenth-century evangelist Billy Sunday. He no doubt observed person after person transformed by the power of the Gospel through Mr. Sunday's ministry, and that became his motivation for writing this hymn:

> Would you be free from the burden of sin?
> There's power in the blood, power in the blood;
> Would you o'er evil a victory win?
> There's wonderful power in the blood.[1]

The power hasn't diminished one iota today. Its power to transform lives is far greater than that of social media, stronger than any addiction, more persuasive than any atheist college professor.

Do you believe it? Of course you do. Do you trust in it enough to put your family in God's hands? That is harder, isn't it? When people I care about are making wrong decisions, I am tempted to want to fix the problem myself rather than rely upon the Gospel. Let me remind you (and me too) to rely on the power of the Gospel; it is *enough* to transform your loved one.

Carol's grandson Drew grew up going to church, but neither she nor his parents saw evidence that he truly trusted in Christ. In fact, through high school, he had become more and more hostile to spiritual things. When he went away to college in another state, they worried that he would reject Christianity entirely. His living in such a secular environment greatly concerned them. They were tempted to try to talk him out of going—to keep him closer to home where they would still have an influence.

Instead, they released him to God's care and began praying that God would draw him to the Gospel. A few months later, grandmother Carol related that his parents began to notice a difference in the questions he asked. "Do you know anything about the churches in this town?" was one of the first.

They listened and watched the Holy Spirit draw him. God put other Christians into his life. He got invited to—and started attending regularly—a Christian group at the college. About a year later, Drew came home and initiated a conversation about spiritual things. In his parents' living room, he told them he knew he wasn't a believer, but he wanted to be. They prayed together, and he trusted Christ as his Savior.

The change was dramatic—many of Drew's old interests disappeared and were replaced with newer, better ones. Today Drew is a godly father and is devoted to his family, his church, and his Lord. He is just one present-day example to me of the power of the Gospel. It has transformed hundreds of millions through the centuries; it certainly has the power to do the same in your family.

Yes, that son-in-law can change. Your broken relationship can be mended. Your grandchildren can survive their parents' divorce. The power of the Gospel is mighty, mighty, mighty— don't forget that!

Because you remember the power that is in the Gospel, you must do three things:

1. *You must trust that power to do its work.* It is a spiritual power that requires God the Holy Spirit's involvement. In fact, real spiritual transformation cannot take place without the Holy Spirit drawing people to Him. You can't be the Holy Spirit yourself—so you can't force the change.

If you haven't already, start praying now that the Holy Spirit will work in the heart of your loved ones and begin drawing them to himself. Pray for other believers to enter their lives, and pray that God would use them.

2. *You must LIVE OUT the Gospel to your loved ones.* And remember, the Gospel is personified as grace. Determine that every interaction, every conversation, is characterized by grace. That's hard, especially if yours is a broken or tense relationship. If that is the case, then pray even harder that you can exemplify God's grace at every opportunity to those in your family. We'll discuss this more in chapter 6.

3. *You must share the truth of the Gospel when you have opportunity.* Don't be the grandparent who just gives up. Don't be the one who wants to avoid conflict and, as a result, avoids talking about spiritual things entirely. In the first chapter I related the story of Gloria, whose son had said, "You may see your granddaughter, or you may talk about God, but you can't do both. The minute you mention God to her, you won't be allowed to see her again."

Here's the next chapter in that story: Gloria honored her son's demands, but she also determined to strengthen the relationship with her granddaughter. During the following summer, she took her granddaughter on a trip to New York City—just the two of them. As they were sightseeing, the granddaughter left her expensive camera in a taxi but didn't discover it was missing until several minutes after the taxi had dropped them off. She was frantic. They called the taxi company, which notified the driver, who said the camera wasn't in his cab. The granddaughter said, "Grandma, let's cross our fingers and hope somebody finds it." Gloria said, "Well, I'm going to pray." (She didn't mention God.)

When they got back to their hotel later that evening and approached the front desk, there was the granddaughter's camera waiting for her! They learned the story from the clerk: The people who got in the cab after them had taken the camera, but then thought better of it. (Gloria says, "Just at the time I was praying.") They called the taxi company, found out where the driver had picked up the passengers before them, and delivered the camera back to the hotel. Gloria was able to tell her granddaughter, "See, prayer works!" (She still didn't mention God). The granddaughter was so impressed—it was likely something she will never forget. The story still isn't finished, but Gloria was certain it was the power of God at work.

Don't you give up either. You will need to wisely select your opportunities to speak up, but pray for opportunities like Gloria's—then let God's Spirit exert His power.

Secret #3: Earnest prayer

Earnest prayer is the method that is a conduit for God's power to be displayed. I love the New Living Translation of James 5:16, which says, "The earnest prayer of a righteous person has great power and produces wonderful results."

This verse has a formula in it: *Earnest prayer + righteous person = great power + wonderful results*. I love that! Those words have given me so much hope, and here are two reasons why.

First of all, this statement is in the book of James, not the book of Romans. Both talk about righteousness, but from a completely different perspective. Romans addresses *positional* righteousness, and says, "There is none righteous, no, not one" (Romans 3:10 KJV). This positional righteousness is synonymous with sinlessness, and so immediately I—and you too—would be disqualified from being able to pray in a way that has great power and produces wonderful results.

But the book of James is about *practical* righteousness, and this kind of righteousness is synonymous with a life that demonstrates faith in God through actions. It doesn't demand perfection, as the meaning in Romans does, but rather genuineness and sincerity. In that case, I can qualify as someone who can pray this way.

Second, it says the "earnest" prayer. I'm so thankful for this word! I've always been a doer, and to be transparent, prayer is one spiritual discipline that I haven't excelled at like I should. I have friends who pray for a half hour every morning; others get "lost" in praying, and a couple of hours go by before they realize it. Still others can pray all night long. I've never been one of those people.

If this verse qualified prayer by time or regularity—"the long prayers of a righteous person," or "the daily prayer"—I'd be sunk. Instead, it says the "earnest" prayer. When I saw this for the first time, I thought, *I can do earnest!* I can be earnest in one prayer. I can be earnest in a short prayer. It means simply that I mean it. No "rote" prayers will do. I believe it means I must clear my mind of other things, and I understand that I am approaching the God of the universe with my conversation. Then, with all sincerity, I give Him my request, knowing that He hears me. Yes, I can do earnest.

Let me remind you (from earlier parts of this chapter) of things to pray earnestly about:

1. Thank God for your position of weakness.
2. Pray that God will accomplish His purpose in you.
3. Pray that the Holy Spirit will begin to draw your loved one to himself.
4. Pray for God to bring other believers into your loved one's life.
5. Pray for the power of the Gospel to be displayed.
6. Pray that everything you do will reflect God's grace.

My friend, start praying this way. It will give you hope. It will lift your spirits. It may just be the means for "great power and wonderful results" to be realized in your family's situation. Just remember—trust in God's wisdom and patiently wait for His timing.

Secret #4: Forgiveness

In every situation where there is hurt, there is likely sin involved as well. Whether it is a broken relationship between grandparent and parent, or the wrong choices of an adult child, the sin in the situation needs to be dealt with.

I've wondered whether, if I recited the Lord's Prayer honestly, I'd pray, "And forgive us our trespasses—but please, Lord, not as I forgive others." I haven't always forgiven others as I should, nor have I always asked for forgiveness when I should.

Here's an example: A few years ago I had to ask another Christian worker to forgive me. Two decades earlier I had chastised him for what I felt was a wrong approach to finances; I had actually taken him to lunch in order to tell him how wrong he was. It took two decades of maturing for me to finally realize that *I* was the one who was wrong. I had been insensitive to his needs and his situation and made a minor issue into a major one. I hadn't seen him in the intervening years—but when I did, the Holy Spirit convicted me that I needed to apologize. Ironically, when I told him I needed to ask for his forgiveness, he didn't even remember the lunch conversation or the issue. *He* didn't need to clear the air, but *I* did. My "repentance" freed me to reestablish a friendship with him that is still growing today. And to top it off, God taught me an important lesson—again.

Could this be why you haven't seen that miracle? Could it be that God might want to do some work in *you* before He displays His power in others? Perhaps a lesson is in His plan for you. Perhaps forgiveness—or asking for it—may very well be Step One toward finding hope for the resolution of the thing that hurts you so much.

Here are three aspects to forgiveness for you to consider.

1. *Asking for forgiveness* for your part in the hurt may be the very thing that will start the healing process. Even if fault is 98 percent theirs to 2 percent yours, you need to ask forgiveness for that 2 percent. Remember, your fault in the problem likely looks much bigger from the other side than it does from yours.

   Asking forgiveness for your part may be the very thing that will start the healing.

   Asking for forgiveness may be really hard to do. I know it can be for me, because it means I must put my ego aside. It means that I must humble myself and—even more difficult—accept that the other person's point of view is completely different from mine and may have validity.

   Don't say, "I'll say I'm sorry when he (or she) does." Be the bigger person. Initiate the reconciliation process by taking the first step. And don't add a condition to the ask. Just take responsibility for any part you might have had in the problem and leave the other party's response to them and God.

   I am urging you—begging you—to consider this important step, if you have not already taken it. Here are some reasons why:

   • *Because you may be wrong*—and you probably are, from the other person's point of view. Remember, in personal relationships, you must deal with perceptions, not reality. "Reality" is what we call our perception, and "delusion" may be what we call the other viewpoint. But the other person may call *us* deluded and believe their point of view to be the truth.

     My good friend Wayne Rice[2] wrote to me about this topic. "One of the most helpful things I have ever learned about conflict resolution is that the other person actually may be right. I don't see it that way; but rather than assign ignorance, or stupidity, or evil intentions to the other person, I have learned it's better to recognize that maybe none of those things are true. They just have a different point of view and it may be entirely valid (from their perspective). In other words, they aren't trying to hurt me. That's an essential understanding, I think, so that healing can take place in my own heart."[3]

- *Because asking forgiveness is commanded in Scripture.* This should go without saying, but I want to draw your attention to the first part of James 5:16 (we just examined the second part): "*Confess your sins to each other and pray for each other so that you may be healed. The earnest prayer of a righteous person has great power and produces wonderful results*" (NLT, emphasis added).

  Notice the "so that"? According to this verse, it is possible that the reason the hurt you are experiencing hasn't been taken away by God ("healed") is because you haven't asked for forgiveness. It is not the *only* reason God doesn't take away hurts, but it is one reason. And it is significant that this exhortation to ask forgiveness immediately precedes the statement concerning earnest prayer.

  Jesus said, in Matthew 5:23–24: "Therefore, if you are offering your gift at the altar and there remember that your brother or sister has something against you, leave your gift there in front of the altar. First go and be reconciled to them; then come and offer your gift."

- *Because asking for forgiveness might be the very thing God uses to start the process toward healing.* Asking for forgiveness disarms; it is the thing that may begin to put cracks in the barrier that is preventing reconciliation.

  Have you asked for forgiveness for any part you have had? If not, plan to do it right away.

2. *Forgiving the offender.* Asking for forgiveness is hard, but forgiving the offense is sometimes harder. In the same email quoted previously, Wayne Rice wrote, "I have found that being able to forgive—completely forgive—my children (or any others who have wronged me) is the key to healing and restoration. That's not easy to do because of grudges, wanting to hold on to being 'right,' etc. But to really let go of pain, you have to let go of the offense and forgive."[4]

3. *Forgetting the offense.* I have marveled many times at what the Old Testament Joseph named his eldest son. Not much is made of the name Manasseh, but it adds such significance to the story of Joseph and his brothers. The naming is recorded in Genesis 41:51:

> Joseph named his firstborn Manasseh and said, "It is because God has made me forget all my trouble and all my father's household."

Manasseh means "forget," or "cause to forget." My take on the story is this: I think getting sold into slavery by your brothers would be hard enough to *forgive* but even harder to *forget.* That is why I marvel at Joseph's statement. Okay—he forgave, but how did he forget such a dastardly deed? Maybe time healed. Maybe the fact that life had gotten good for Joseph helped. Maybe the birth of his firstborn was what did it—in any case, Joseph had managed to get beyond merely forgiving: He *forgot* this terrible thing that had happened to him.

There was a time that a serious crime was committed upon a member of our family. I remember so well the rage that would well up in me for months, even years after. I struggled— *hard*—with forgiving the offender. I knew I should as a Christian, but oh, it was so difficult. I finally gained victory over the anger by determining to choose to forgive anew every morning if I needed to. I share this to illustrate that I understand how difficult it is to forgive. But *forgetting*—that is ever so much harder than forgiving. I'm not sure I have mastered that even today. That is why I marvel at Joseph: He not only *forgave*, he *forgot*!

That is also what is so amazing about how God forgives—Isaiah 43:25 makes it clear: "I, even I, am he who blots out your transgressions, for my own sake, and remembers your sins no more."

"Remembers your sins *no more*." We don't have the power to erase things from our memory—but God does. And while we may not have the ability to hit Delete on things in our conscious memory, we can *treat* the hurts as if we have forgotten them. We can choose to not let them have any power over us. We can choose to stop letting them affect our attitudes and our actions. That's what Joseph did with his brothers' despicable deed.

Are you holding on to the *memory* of that thing, that event, those words that hurt? Take it from me: forget them. Determine to remember the sin *no more*. Then, when you do remember the hurt (and you will), choose to forget again. You will not be sorry, and you will find incredible healing and amazing power in doing so.

Comfort from Scripture

- This has been the life verse of my wife, Diane, and there's not been a single time in our lives when it has not proven to be good advice: "Trust in the Lord with all your heart and lean not on your own understanding; in all your ways submit to him, and he will make your paths straight" (Proverbs 3:5–6).
- You've seen God do mighty things, haven't you? And He likely isn't done displaying His power in your life. Take note

of those mighty things; you are going to want to declare them to your grandchildren: "Even when I am old and gray, do not forsake me, my God, till I declare your power to the next generation, your mighty acts to all who are to come" (Psalm 71:18).

- You can do it! Today, determine that you will trust in what this verse says: "Ah, Sovereign Lord, you have made the heavens and the earth by your great power and outstretched arm. Nothing is too hard for you" (Jeremiah 32:17).

- Meditate on God's forgiveness: Psalm 103:12 says that "as far as the east is from the west, so far has he removed our transgressions from us." How can you be a model of how God forgives in your situation?

Questions to ponder

1. Have you wished for a miracle in your situation, and secretly been disappointed that it didn't happen when you wanted it to?

2. How do you react to the apostle Paul's attitude toward weakness—that he delights in it? Have you reached that point in your dependence upon God?

3. How have you viewed the trial you face in your family? Have you been able to see it as an opportunity for God to display His power?

4. To be more effective in living out the Gospel in front of your family, what do you need to change?

5. How have you been praying for your family trial? Considering what you read in this chapter, how will you pray differently from now on?

6. Do you need to forgive, forget, or ask for forgiveness? What might be your first step to take?

5

The Influence Principle

What do you do when there is *relational* distance? At the beginning of the book I shared Caren and Tom's story of alienation from their grandchildren—when their former daughter-in-law cut off all communication. Here's another instance:

Garry and Val said they couldn't get close to their grandkids because the parents wouldn't let them. The reason? Their daughter (the mom) said they were just too busy. Both their daughter and their son-in-law had demanding jobs that left them exhausted by the weekend, and that resulted in them not going to church. That concerned Garry and Val, but their greater concern was that the parents didn't want visitors. "We are just too tired to have company" was their response when Val tried to schedule a visit. Garry and Val felt powerless. They wanted to have more of a relationship with their grandchildren but felt stymied by the parents' busyness.

Garry and Val needed to figure out a new strategy to get past this barrier to regular connection with their grandchildren. My recommendation was to examine what they were doing (remember, we can't change others, only ourselves) based upon what I call *the influence principle*.

A number of years ago I wrote a book called *Raising a Modern-Day Joseph*. I began the book this way:

> Parenting in a real sense is the process of letting go. When our little baby comes home from the hospital, we start with complete control of that baby's life; but we also begin letting go. First, it's letting them sit up without support. In a few months, it's letting them walk around the coffee table. It's like we have this tight, controlling grip at the beginning, and then we gradually start letting go, one finger at a time. For most parents, loosening each finger is difficult.
>
> Sending a child to kindergarten is a difficult moment. You're controlling with only nine fingers now, or maybe eight. Years later, another big challenge is allowing your child to drive alone for the first time at age sixteen or seventeen. By then your grip is down to three or four fingers, if that.
>
> But when you completely open that last finger, finally releasing your child to his own decisions, his own common sense, his own wisdom—that's the toughest. It's what I call the MDM, the Most Difficult Moment.[1]

I wrote that book before I began thinking much about the grand-parenting role. I hadn't really considered what happens *after* a parent releases control of his child—when that child becomes a young adult, and then a parent himself. I'd now add another Most Difficult Moment—the moment in which we learn the adult child has made a bad decision and we can't do anything to fix it. We'd like to, but we feel powerless to step in.

Sometimes we try, but it only messes things up more. *We* create relational distance through an unwise approach to *their* life choices. In this chapter, I'm asking you to think through your approach and consider a better one. If you've attempted to intervene in a bad decision your adult child has made, and that attempt hasn't been welcomed, leaving your relationship cool or worse—ice-cold—I have an approach for you to consider. I call it the *influence principle*. Here's the simple precept:

> *Control comes through (parental) authority;*
> *influence comes through a relationship.*

Controlling as part of parenting

Wise parenting means that as the childhood years go by, the level of control begins to go down and down and down. As I stated in the quote from *Raising a Modern-Day Joseph*, control starts out high, but over the course of raising your children, you gradually release them to their own independence.

When they are in their later teen years, control is at a minimum. It is actually a wise, natural progression, but it probably happened whether you intended it to or not. Releasing control is necessary to having a responsible, independent adult. After all, nobody wants a forty-five-year-old still living at home, entirely dependent on Mom and Dad.

How much control does that mean you have now? *Zero.*

However, when our adult children make bad decisions, the parent in us wants to regain control—we want to fix whatever needs fixing. And if we attempt to control our adult child, the result is quite predictable: damage.

However, control is not the whole picture. There's another ingredient in the process of raising a child, and that is *influence*. It starts this way: With a brand-new baby, you have a lot of control, but you don't have too much influence. Our youngest grandchild,

two-year-old Micah, responds better to discipline than to reason. His parents must exert control, but they want to increase influence at the same time.

If you are a wise parent, control will go down as you progress through the childhood years, but

influence should go up. Of course you will impact your children through control at the beginning, and then more and more through influence as they get older.

Controlling and grandparenting

What does all this have to do with grandparenting? A lot—because the role of a grandparent is different from that of a parent. According to most theologians' thinking, Genesis 2:24 establishes marriage: "That is why a man leaves his father and mother and is united to his wife, and they become one flesh." Most focus on "a man" and "his wife," and point out that this verse describes a new relationship that forms the foundation for marriage. But it *also* means a new relationship for the father and mother—they no longer have the same relationship with, or control over, their son and the new family.

That means you must interact differently with your adult child than you did when they were in your home. In fact, here are seven things to work on:

1. *Let go of control.* As a grandparent, you have already released control, and you shouldn't be trying to take it back. It is certainly a temptation when things go wrong, but you *mustn't* do so—unless you are invited. Think of the sign illustrations above. The two factors—control and influence—are like two ends of a seesaw. When one goes up, the other

has to go down. When you "up" the control, what happens to influence? It goes down. Your son or daughter will resent the approach, and the wall between you will only grow higher. If you want to "up" the influence, control has to go down.

2. *Identify controlling responses.* "But I don't control," you say. Are you sure? Controlling likely looks different than it did when our kids were in our homes. On the adult level, it looks like criticism, sharing our opinion even though it is not asked for, or trying to "guilt" the other person. Nonverbal behaviors such as not listening, the silent treatment, or negative body language can be tools to try to control as well. Have you been unknowingly (or maybe knowingly) using controlling behaviors? If you have, how has that worked? Has it been effective? Maybe it's time to change your approach.

   Here are three controlling responses that don't work well:

   a. **Attempting to re-parent.** We think, *They should listen to us—after all, we are their parent.* But when we step back into that role, we risk further alienation.

   b. **Blaming or guilt-tripping.** Your son or daughter likely already feels guilty for the wrong decisions, or what has caused the broken relationship. But you may need to let the Holy Spirit bring on the guilt rather than you doing it, especially if your relationship is not what it should be.

   c. **Justifying our position.** "See, I was right," aka "I told you so" rarely brings a good result. So no matter how right you are, avoid making this kind of a controlling statement.

3. *Understand what produces influence.* Influence comes through a different channel than control does. *Control* comes through *authority*—real or perceived—but *influence* comes through a

relationship. In fact, the better the relationship you have with your adult children and their spouses, the greater the influence you will have with them.

When you had your child in your home, you rightfully had *parental authority*—and therefore, parental control. Now that your child has become an adult, you have relinquished that authority and control, and it doesn't work to try to take it back. Doing so *diminishes* influence, rather than increasing it.

While you are still the parent (noun), in most cases you should no longer parent (verb) unless invited.

However, in a healthy relationship, influence builds through the years as a relationship builds. Influence replaces control as the most effective means of impacting our children. Were you dissuaded from doing wrong when you were a teenager simply because you didn't want your parents to be disappointed? Many of us were. It's good to ask, "Why was that effective?" The answer likely is that the relationship was strong between you and your parents.

4. *Evaluate the effectiveness of your influence.* It is directly proportional to the depth of your relationship. A healthy, strong relationship results in much influence, and an injured, shallow, or nonexistent relationship will result in little or no influence. Do you see? When you try to revert back to parenting (i.e., controlling), you injure the relationship, resulting in less influence.

A new strategy

I would ask you to think and pray about this. *God, is there a different approach I might take?* You've likely told others that stupidity is doing the same thing and expecting different results. Maybe it is now time to apply that wisdom yourself—to examine the strategy you have used so far and change it. If your response to your adult child's wrong decisions has been to parent again (control), it is time for a new strategy—an *influence* strategy.

Since you are no longer in a position to control, you can look to many passages of Scripture that give guidance about how to respond. May I suggest 1 Corinthians 13:4–8? Notice how many of the phrases are relational in nature:

> Love is patient, love is kind. It does not envy, it does not boast, it is not proud. It does not dishonor others, it is not self-seeking, it is not easily angered, it keeps no record of wrongs. Love does not delight in evil but rejoices with the truth. It always protects, always trusts, always hopes, always perseveres. Love never fails.

This passage, all about relationship, gives the backdrop for a new strategy to create influence. Look at it again: *Patience* produces influence opportunities. *Kindness* produces influence opportunities. So do humility, selflessness, and being even-tempered. An absence of revenge, a refusal to gossip—everything mentioned in this passage will create opportunities to impact through relationships. Keep it in mind as you follow the next steps to build your new strategy:

5. *Double your efforts to reestablish the relationship.* Identify what's causing the break in the relationship—remember, the effectiveness of your attempts to positively influence will be directly proportional to the depth of your relationship. *So how deep is the relationship?*

    Let me urge you: Don't give up! You are their *parent*. The potential is still there for a great relationship—and great influence. Never stop reaching out; never stop loving.

    Remember, God continues to relentlessly pursue people no matter how they respond to Him. That was Jesus' purpose in coming to earth: "For the Son

The effectiveness of your influence is directly proportional to the depth of your relationship.

of Man came to seek and to save the lost" (Luke 19:10). If He does that with His children, we ought to do the same with ours.

It may help you to write it out. Take a sheet of paper and make two columns. List on the left what you have done to weaken or damage the relationship, then what your son or daughter has done on the right. You'll probably write fast and furiously on the right side but much more slowly and reluctantly on the left. In fact, you may have difficulty thinking of anything to write in your column. If that is the case, stop the process and take time to pray and ask God to reveal to you what you might have done to contribute to the breakdown. You're wise enough to know that in nearly every conflict there is liability on both sides, so don't stop until you have some things in your column.

Then, in the right-hand column (theirs), write, "I can't change these" across the column. In the left-hand column (yours), write, "Work on these." Remember, you cannot change others, so focus on your own heart.

6. *Expect any change to take time.* The deeper the hurt, the longer it may take for the relationship to be restored. If your hurt involves a son-in-law or a daughter-in-law, it may be that you have never had a relationship to begin with. And it may be that you don't really like each other. It may be that they don't want a relationship, which will make the process even harder.

Consider Jesus' example: He desired a relationship with us, even when we didn't want one. He loved us when we were unlovable and didn't want loving. He patiently waits and draws us until we desire a relationship with Him. Can you "live out Jesus" to that one you are so concerned about?

7. *Focus on constructive connections.* Even if it is a sports team or a hobby or a store you like to shop in—anything that will

form a basis for connecting will do for a start. If you have a broken relationship with your adult child, then think, *What is a constructive connection I might have with them that we might work together on to begin to build a friendship?* Let the more important stuff go for a while—until the relationship is rebuilt. You might then be invited to speak to the issues that concern you.

It is easy for us to think, *My son-in-law is not this. He's not that . . . My daughter is not doing this. She's not doing that.* All this does is make us want to control them more. If we focus instead on how we can connect with that son-in-law or that daughter, we will be less tempted to control and more likely to do the things that will result in a deepening relationship and eventual influence.

Instead, think, *What can I do so they will listen to me and welcome my advice?* Remember, advice that is not asked for is almost always taken as criticism. As parents, we are naturally tempted to do what we did when they were kids—try to control those impulses. When they were children and they did something wrong, we punished. Wouldn't we like to do that with our adult kids sometimes? But we don't have the right to anymore because we've released control. Therefore we have to change our tactics and focus on relationships instead.

Gregg and Angie wanted to meet us for coffee. As they sat with Diane and me, they shared their hurt: their relationship with their daughter was really struggling. As we talked through this control-influence principle, Gregg realized that he had been trying to resolve the break in the relationship with a controlling approach. As we talked about restoring the relationship and focusing on influence, we could literally see the hope come back to their faces. We talked about how they might begin restoring the relationship—being ready to ask forgiveness, listening, and expressing their desire to mend the hurts. A couple weeks later I received a message from Gregg. It was short but so affirming: He shared how they had reached out to their daughter, who agreed to meet with them and have a conversation. They were so excited because they felt that the door to a better relationship had cracked open. Progress had been made.

Your ministry to your family

I have a final thought for you, Christian grandparent, regarding this issue of relationships. Your ministry in this world, according to Scripture, can be described in one word: *reconciliation*. Second Corinthians 5:18–20 is the basis:

> All this is from God, who reconciled us to himself through Christ and gave us the ministry of reconciliation: that God was reconciling the world to himself in Christ, not counting people's sins against them. And he has committed to us the message of reconciliation. We are therefore Christ's ambassadors, as though God were making his appeal through us. We implore you on Christ's behalf: Be reconciled to God.

The word *reconcile* in its various forms appears five times. Three times it refers to God's work of saving us and restoring us into a relationship with Him. Twice it refers to what we are to do: He *"gave us the ministry of reconciliation"* and *"committed to us the message of reconciliation."*

Your ministry can be described in one word: reconciliation.

Reconciliation—restoring the relationship—describes what Christ did in His death and resurrection. It is also what you, as a Christian, must pursue for your family. It is Job Number One for you. Give it all you've got, because reconciliation in your family may be the very thing that opens the door to your family members being reconciled to God.

Challenge from Scripture

- Inner peace, and peace in relationships. Those two concepts are to characterize us as Christ-followers: "Let the peace of Christ rule in your hearts, since as members of one body you were called to peace. And be thankful" (Colossians 3:15).

- The center section of the love chapter is so applicable to relationships. Meditate on each phrase as it applies to your family: "Love is patient, love is kind. It does not envy, it does not boast, it is not proud. It does not dishonor others, it is not self-seeking, it is not easily angered, it keeps no record of wrongs. Love does not delight in evil but rejoices with the truth. It always protects, always trusts, always hopes, always perseveres. Love never fails" (1 Corinthians 13:4–8).

Questions to ponder

1. How do you react to the principle, "Control comes through (parental) authority, influence comes through a relationship"?

2. Have you released control of your adult children? What controlling behaviors are most tempting to you?

3. Describe your relationship with someone who has been a great influence in your life. What can you learn from that experience that might help you with your family relationships?

4. If you need to reestablish a relationship or strengthen one, what do you think are going to be your first steps toward that goal?

5. Will you need to ask forgiveness for your part in a broken relationship? If so, how are you going to do that?

6. *Reconciliation* is a word that describes your ministry to your family. Does that sound exciting to you or daunting? Or would you pick another word to describe your reaction?

6

The Grace Strategy

The adult class I was teaching at my church was discussing the research concerning young adults who had walked away from their faith practice, if not their beliefs. Then it turned from a fairly sterile discussion about the national situation to a "God moment."

It began with Dave's eyes welling up with tears. He blurted out, "Larry, I'm one for three." What he meant was that of his three children, only one was following God. Another dad identified with him: "Don't feel bad, I'm zero for two." Still another father offered, "I'm two for four." They all started sharing—transparently—the struggles they were having with their own children's spiritual walk. Quickly it began to hit home—the national statistics were not about another denomination, another part of the country, or the church that was having problems—they reflected *my* class, *my* friends. The reality was that a majority of my class, my friends, were experiencing deep pain because some of our own children had become prodigals.

Grandparent, if you have an adult child who has walked away from their faith, you are not alone. I believe there are millions who share your heartache in our country. You are not alone in your church, and probably not alone in your class or small group. Yet we rarely reveal this greatest hurt of life. We are simply too hurt—or maybe too embarrassed—to talk about it much.

If you have an adult child who is not walking with God, this chapter is for you. You'll receive hope as you think through how to respond in a way that Jesus did, mirroring His example to those who were "sinners."

You're the only Jesus

I'd like to establish an assumption: If you have an adult child who is not walking with God, that son or daughter has likely cut off relationships with other Christians. As I have interacted with dozens of grandparents in this situation, they almost always validate the truth of that by saying something like, "Yes, they've left all their Christian friends." That means you're likely the only "Jesus representative" in their circle of contacts, and you are there because you are family.

What does it mean to "be Jesus" to them? To answer that, we look to John 1:14—the conclusion of that marvelous beginning of the Gospel of John:

> The Word became flesh and made his dwelling among us. We have seen his glory, the glory of the one and only Son, who came from the Father, full of grace and truth.

If you've been a regular churchgoer for any length of time, I'm sure you have heard a sermon about this verse and you know that, when the last part of the verse says "full of grace and truth," it doesn't mean 80 percent grace and 20 percent truth. It doesn't mean Jesus was 50 percent truth and 50 percent grace. What it means is that Jesus was *full* of grace and *full* of truth. He was 100 percent grace and 100 percent truth, the complete embodiment of both.

However, we can't possibly be complete truth and complete grace, because we are sinful. Yet He's our example and we want to be like Him, don't we? So we want to be as truthful as we can be and as grace-filled as we can be.

However, I encourage you to think about another question that I believe will help you:

"Being Jesus" to my family means I am the embodiment of grace and truth!

Jesus' strategy

What was Jesus' *strategy*? What did He lead with—grace or truth? When our Savior—this personification of truth and the personification of grace—dealt with other people, did He start with truth, or did He start with grace?

- *With His disciples*, He often led with truth. He told Peter, "Get behind me, Satan."[1] It doesn't appear to me that Jesus was leading in this situation with grace; instead, He immediately confronted Peter with truth. Why would Jesus lead with truth with His disciples? *Because they were ready to receive it.* He had a close relationship with the twelve, and they had already received grace—so it was appropriate to speak truth.

- *With the Pharisees*, Jesus also often led with truth. "You brood of vipers!"[2] also isn't a grace-first approach. Why would He speak this way to Pharisees? Because they were religious hypocrites, possibly, who needed to be shocked and challenged with the error of their own beliefs.

- *With sinners*, He led with grace. This change in strategy is significant, and it is worthy of our close examination. If your son or daughter is living a life of sin in their actions, or has rejected the truth of Scripture, you will do well to consider adopting a similar strategy in your interactions and relationship with them.

One of the greatest examples of this is the woman caught in adultery in John chapter 8. Remember that story? Here is how it begins:

> The teachers of the law and the Pharisees brought in a woman caught in adultery. They made her stand before the group and said to Jesus, "Teacher, this woman was caught in the act of adultery. In the Law Moses commanded us to stone such women. Now what do you say?"[3]

While they had underlying motives (the next verse makes that clear), the teachers and Pharisees were asking Jesus to pronounce truth. They led with what they believed to be truth themselves: "This woman was caught in the act of adultery," and, "Moses commanded us to stone such women."

Then they asked Jesus to also pronounce truth: "Now what do you say?" But Jesus refused to answer in the way they wanted. Instead, He had a different approach.

> But Jesus bent down and started to write on the ground with his finger.[4]

I've wondered what He wrote. Maybe it was the names of some women the accusers had messed around with. Whatever it was, it caused them to shrink away, one by one:

> At this, those who heard began to go away one at a time, the older ones first, until only Jesus was left, with the woman still standing there.[5]

Jesus then addressed the woman. He could have then spoken only the hard, punishing truth. He could have said, "Woman, you *did* commit adultery," or, "The Law *does* say that adulterers are to be executed." But instead He spoke words of grace:

> Jesus straightened up and asked her, "Woman, where are they? Has no one condemned you?"

"No one, sir," she said.

"Then neither do I condemn you," Jesus declared. [6]

In fact, everything Jesus had done and said to that point was grace-filled. He no doubt knew that now she would be able to receive truth, so this scene ends with Him speaking stark truth to the woman:

"Go now and leave your life of sin."[7]

Jesus, who was the full embodiment of both grace and truth, sometimes led with truth so people would receive grace. At other times, He led with grace so people would receive truth.

Grandparent, what has your strategy been to this point? Have you, with your adult child who is not walking with God, led with truth or with grace?

Our generation grew up in churches that elevated truth, and I'm glad they did. We've passionately believed in the truth of God's Word; we've gone to conferences on truth, heard dozens of sermons on truth, and proclaimed truth to our world. We know words like *inerrancy*, *infallibility*, and *inspiration*. We are "truth" pros. In reflecting back, though, I've often wondered if we have done a good job of balancing that truth with grace. I've wondered if we should have been more discerning and led with grace more often so that people would hear truth.

I was teaching a workshop on this topic of dealing with prodigal adult children. A lady raised her hand and said, "You know what I do? I just tell my son, 'The Bible says . . .'" She thought it was a great answer, because she likely had been taught to respond to challenges to her faith with truth. I asked her, "So how has that worked?" My question stopped her. "Well . . ." (Long pause.) "So far it hasn't." I encouraged her to consider leading with grace instead.

Let me make it clear: I am not suggesting that you neglect truth, or even diminish truth. We must do neither. However, neither must we neglect or diminish *grace*. My many conversations on this subject tell me that when we grandparent-types get grace and truth out of balance, we usually err on the side of pushing truth and neglecting grace.

However, you who err on the other side—who don't speak the truth and think you are being gracious by staying silent and keeping the peace—you also should consider your approach in light of Jesus' example. He was clear with His assessment of the adulterous woman's behavior: He called it sin, and He told her to do it "no more," as many translations put it. What if He had never made this last statement? He would have neglected truth. His example is helpful for those who are tempted to remain silent when we should speak the truth in love.

I want to give you grandparents who are struggling with a wayward child hope through a new strategy. It is a really good one, because it is Jesus' strategy: *Lead with grace!* "Okay," you say, "so what does that look like?" Let's first define what leading with truth may look or sound like.

Leading with truth

What does leading with truth mean? It can look like teaching, or mentoring. Think of Jesus' sermons and His conversations with His disciples. For us, it means communicating what we know or believe to be true through statements, conversation, or other means.

Leading with truth is exactly the right approach in many occasions. Our adult children can be blinded by emotion, or unhealthily influenced by bad friends. They can be in the process of making unwise decisions, and when that is the case, it is appropriate that we speak up. Such a strategy is born out of our deep love for them and our concern for their welfare and future. Here's an example:

Joe and Teri's young-adult daughter was involved in and blind to what they saw as a destructive, dead-end relationship with a married man. She accepted the man's proposal and made plans to marry him once his divorce was final. As Joe and Teri described their journey to help her see the truth, I hurt with them. They told of the despair they felt as the wedding date drew nearer: Their daughter was about to make a horrible, life-impacting decision. They told of praying with all their might. They fasted. They described how they tried to get her to see the truth of the situation. Teri in particular had persisted in speaking truth to her daughter, urging her to think again. Finally, one week before the wedding date, their daughter finally heard what they had been saying and called off the wedding. Their prayers were answered, and their determination to speak truth with their daughter was rewarded.

Their situation was one in which leading with truth was entirely appropriate; doing so resulted in their daughter avoiding a terrible decision and possibly a terrible future. However, in less urgent matters, our "leading with truth" may look different to the one on the receiving end of our truth statements, depending on their state of mind.

To someone receptive to the truth or the truth-giver, it may look informative and insightful, and they receive it gladly. With someone not ready to receive it, the same information may seem opinionated and manipulative, and they react negatively against it. Let's examine a couple of phrases grandparents may use with their adult children:

> *"You really should be . . . (going to church, etc.)."* Is this true? Yes, our adult child really should be going to church. It is a truth statement. We lead with a truth statement like this because we are the parents and we are used to telling them what they need to do. It can be a control statement that is meant to motivate them through guilt. On the other hand, urging them to do the right thing, when they are ready to hear it, can be "speaking the truth in love."
>
> How have your attempts to instruct them been received thus far? If they are rejecting you, continuing to use the same

strategy might make the relational barrier higher and make them more resistant to conversations about spiritual things. Such an approach is usually counterproductive and doesn't accomplish what we want.

"You need to understand . . ." Statements like this are belittling. They also may be an attempt on our part to elevate our opinions into truth statements. After all, we all *think* our opinions are true, don't we? When we push our opinions on others and portray a demeanor that they must be accepted as truth, we only create resistance, shut down communication, and injure relationships.

There are many times when we need to lead with truth. But if that is what you have been attempting and you are not seeing the results you want in your adult child, change your approach and consider leading with grace.

Leading with grace

What does it mean to lead with grace? Grace means "undeserved favor." Consider those two words: first, *undeserved*. That adult child who is the reason you are reading this book may deserve to hear the truth; they may deserve a response to their comments. Grace means you will withhold what is deserved for what is undeserved. Second, *favor*. Favor is positive; it is for the good of the person on the receiving end.

That's why grace is not the silent treatment—but it may be silence. Silent treatment is used to punish; silence can be used to buy time, to listen, to try to understand, and to think of the best response. Think back to the story of Jesus and the woman caught in adultery. He *led* with silence. He wasn't quick to share truth, because He no doubt recognized that the woman needed to get in the right frame of mind to receive it, and leading with grace was the perfect way to achieve that.

Therefore, sometimes grace sounds like silence. *Listening.* Trying to understand. I'm reminding myself of this as I write, because I am naturally wired to quickly contribute verbally to a conversation. I'm often guilty of sharing my opinion too quickly. Are you like me? Then join me in a recommitment to lead with grace more often in relationships.

Sometimes the very best way to lead with grace is to say, "Please forgive me." Saying those three words is difficult enough when you clearly have been at fault. But what if you haven't been at fault? Or maybe just a tiny bit? In almost every argument and conflict there is culpability on both sides, even when it might be that 2 percent to 98 percent we discussed back in chapter 4. Consider what percentage your son or daughter would use to assign responsibility to you for what has happened. If it's anything over zero, then I encourage you to consider leading with the words, "Please forgive me." Remember, if you feel they don't deserve to hear you say those words, then saying them fits perfectly into the definition of grace.

Did you ever say something like, "You're not part of our family," "You're not the daughter I raised," "You have brought shame to our family name"? Statements like this can cause long-term, lingering hurt. If you've ever said them in the past, a good way for you to show grace would be to start by asking forgiveness for those words.

Loving them as they are is leading with grace. Jamie and Rick's son Trevor had been in and out of prison, had had various addictions in his young adult years, and fathered their only grandson. Trevor couldn't keep a job and had let his personal appearance go. "How can he continue to make such sinful choices when we raised him to follow God?" his parents wondered often. Prim-and-proper Jamie admitted she was repulsed by his choice of clothing and his unkempt appearance—"I never dreamed my son would look like that." But she and Rick were determined to love Trevor unconditionally. "If we don't, who will?" Rick shared. The story of the prodigal son was an inspiration for them. "We want to be like the father in the story," Rick told me. "No matter what new pigpen Trevor has been in, our arms will always be open to him." And while Trevor hadn't yet come back to Christ, they were beginning to see hopeful signs in some "searching" questions that he had asked.

What would leading with grace look like for you? Maybe it is refusing to remember a past hurt, or avoiding the temptation to bring up a painful subject.

Maybe it is sincerely trying to understand. Remember at the beginning of the book I told you about Janice, who came up to me after a teaching session on grandparenting and said that her three children had all converted to Buddhism? She wondered what to do, and frankly, I didn't have a good answer for her.

We lead with grace so others will accept truth. We lead with truth so others will accept grace.

A number of months later, I was sharing my passion with a group of leaders and staff members at Focus on the Family. Included in the group were some veteran family counselors. One approached me afterward and said, "Do you know what I would have told that mom?" I was hooked.

"No, what?" "I'd have told her, 'Start learning about Buddhism.'"

What he said was so insightful—and significant. He *didn't* say, "Convert to Buddhism." He was saying that his advice to the mother would have been, "Try to understand." Remember, understanding does not mean you are in agreement. But it may position you and equip you to be much more effective when the opportunity arises to share truth.

A visual exercise

Take a break from reading for a moment and stand up.

Okay, you're standing up, correct? Next, get in a running position—not like a sprinter does, but like you did when you ran a race in grade school.

Now, look down at your feet—which one is in front? Your right or your left? I've discovered, when I've had audiences do this, that there is a pretty good balance between those of us who put the right foot forward and those who put the left foot forward.

Whichever is in front, point to that one and say, "This is my truth foot." Now switch feet—put the other one in front. How does it feel? Off-balance? Awkward? Weird? It does for most people.

Point to the one that is now in front and say, "This is my grace foot." Once you've done that, you can sit down and get back to reading.

This exercise illustrates that our natural tendency is to put truth out there and lead with that—because after all, we're the parent! We've told them before, and our natural tendency is to tell them again.

I urge you—consider trying a strategy that is going to feel awkward because it is not natural. You are going to have to think about it for it to work. *Lead with grace*—try it!

A final summary

Some of you have an adult child who for years has resisted your efforts to get them to see the truth. So what if you decided that for years you are going to lead with grace? That might be so hard! But if what you are doing right now is not working, how about trying the Jesus way and treating sinners the way He did? Lead with grace—it works!

Christian grandparent, are you as passionate about dispensing grace to *others* as you are thankful that God gave *you* grace? Be Jesus to that wayward son or daughter. Love them as they are. Lead with grace—it may just be the strategy God uses to bring them back to Him.

Before we get to a list of practical ideas in the final chapter, let's summarize the strategy from this chapter and the last:

Work on strengthening relationships so you have influence.

Build that influence so you will be able to be heard.

Let grace lead until they are ready to hear the truth.

Challenge from Scripture

- "One who loves a pure heart and who speaks with grace will have the king for a friend" (Proverbs 22:11).
- Consider what it might mean to live in the grace of Christ, keeping in mind the situation with your adult children: "I am astonished that you are so quickly deserting the one who called you to live in the grace of Christ and are turning to a different gospel—which is really no gospel at all" (Galatians 1:6–7).
- "Let your conversation be always full of grace, seasoned with salt, so that you may know how to answer everyone" (Colossians 4:6).

Questions to ponder

1. Have you ever tried to lead with truth and it didn't work as you thought it would? Why do you think it didn't work?
2. Have you ever led with truth and it *did* work? What were the factors that made it accomplish what you wanted?
3. What are your observations about Jesus' strategy in dealing with the woman caught in adultery (John 8)? Why do you think He didn't merely pronounce truth to her?
4. What has been your strategy in dealing with your prodigal son or daughter? Have you been leading with truth or with grace?
5. Obviously, the premise of this chapter is that grandparents should adopt a strategy of leading with grace. Look back through the suggestions given, and think through what that might look like in your situation.

7

Give Me Some Practical Ideas!

Every hurt that grandparents experience has its own special set of circumstances. This book has focused on biblical principles, ways of thinking, and strategies to overcome these grandparenting barriers. This final chapter will give you practical ideas to help. Listed below are specific things you can do to deal with each particular situation.

When grandkids live far away

This most-common barrier to intentional grandparenting stymies many grandparents. Below are three ideas, but if you have grandkids who live a distance away, check out the many more ideas in the book *Long-Distance Grandparenting* by Wayne Rice, which is part of this GRANDPARENTING MATTERS series.

1. *Communicate as much as you can.* Of course, there are lots of factors—the age of the grandkids, their schedule, your schedule, and don't forget the parents' perception on this.

Our smartphones, tablets, and computers have made this so much easier than it was a generation ago, haven't they? You probably know how to connect by video, and that's our best recommendation. One grandma told us she has breakfast with her seven-year-old granddaughter every Saturday morning—even though the grandma lives in the U.S. and the granddaughter lives in Sweden. It means that Grandma has to have her "breakfast" on Friday evening, but that is a small price to pay for the privilege of regular communication. Another grandmother communicated the old-fashioned way, and sent her granddaughter a postcard every week for all four years that she was at college. The granddaughter kept them all; they became a very precious memory for her.

2. *Communicate in the way that is best for the grandkids.* That differs according to the age of the grandkids, but don't expect your grandkids to enter "grandparent world"—you need to enter theirs. That means you must text. Keep them engaged—share jokes (there are some great websites for grandkid jokes), ask questions, and make your texts about them and their life. However, like the grandma above—don't forget old-fashioned "snail mail." Receiving something personal in the mail is rare for kids today, so that can become very special to them.

Don't expect your grandkids to enter "grandparent world"— you need to enter theirs!

3. *Have a "grand date" with each one* when visiting. Don't just have adult time, or even family time—have individual time. Make it special—take them out for ice cream or coffee or a long walk. You will find that the grandkids will share things with you that they would never share in the family setting. You'll probably get to talk with them about some pretty serious stuff. One caution: Make sure you listen. You want them to enjoy it so they will want to do it again, so get them

talking about themselves and their interests. And don't come into the "date" with a long list of things you want to say; instead, pick one significant thing you want to share with them, and do that.

4. *"Adopt" a grandkid from your church or community.* If you don't have a good outlet for all that grandparent energy and passion, I *guarantee* there are children who could benefit greatly from your wisdom, attention, and influence. Diane and I have done that: We asked a single mom if her kids could use a "church grandma and grandpa." The mom was eager for us to help—her children had only one other grandparent involved in their lives. We began doing the things that grandparents would do with her kids, and it gave us opportunities to have input into the mom's life as well. Ask the children's leadership team at your church who might need such help and attention; you will both benefit greatly!

When your grandkids are impacted by their parents' divorce

Your relationship with your grandchildren has likely changed dramatically by the divorce: either you stepped into your grandchildren's lives with significantly more frequency, or you have been shut out. Here are some things to remember when you are in the middle of all the drama:

1. *Make your home a safe place for your grandchildren.* They need to have somewhere they can go where there is stability, peace, and unconditional love. You as grandparents can provide that when their own home may be in turmoil. That means not bringing up the divorce if you can keep from doing so. The only exception is if the grandchild brings it up and wants to talk about it.

    While they are at your house, fill your grandchildren's time with active things—and do them together if you can.

Physical activity is always therapeutic for stress, and you will serve your grandkids well with a hike, a game of catch, or whatever fits their interests.

2. *Don't put down either of the parents.* If you do have a talk with your grandchildren about the divorce, speak of both their mom and their dad with respect. You likely take your own child's side in this mess, but remember that the other parent is still *their* parent, and you will injure your relationship with the grands by speaking badly of one of their parents.

"Do not let any unwholesome talk come out of your mouths, but only what is helpful for building others up according to their needs, that it may benefit those who listen" (Ephesians 4:29).

3. *Embrace the significant relationship change that has happened to you.* Many of you have already or will become a secondary caregiver because of a divorce, and it will impact your strength, your pocketbook, and your schedule immensely. Look at this as if God is saying, "I want you to give more time to your legacy in your family"—and thank Him for the opportunity to be light in darkness, to demonstrate His grace and healing to a family damaged by lots of pain.

Others of you will find your contact with your grandchildren greatly diminished, possibly even cut off completely. I encourage you to be patient. Respond with love and grace to the best of your ability, and pray *earnestly* that God will change the mind of the parent who is denying you access. In time, many situations similar to yours improve. Remember that God promises *all things work together for good*—and even this painful chaos your family is in right now is something He can use! *Don't give up!*

4. *Put together a photo album*, either physical or digital, of the good times you had before the divorce. Be sensitive to your

adult child's wishes concerning photos of the ex-spouse. Often, family pictorial records are destroyed one way or another through a messy divorce, and you may be the only one preserving the memories in that way. There will come a time when such mementos will be meaningful to your grandchildren—I promise you.

When you can't contact your grandkids at all

We grandparents are sometimes shut out for reasons that are entirely out of our control—including divorce. Sometimes, we have contributed unknowlingly to an escalating tension in the relationship with our adult children that ends up in a complete severing of the relationship.

1. *Of course, pray.* Pray regularly, and don't let your discouragement over not seeing them impact how diligently you pray for them.

2. *Respect the parents' wishes.* You will further erode trust by attempting to circumvent the restrictions they have put on contact. Instead, think about how you can regain trust that might result in the parents relaxing their prohibitions.

3. *Keep a journal of your thoughts and prayers for them.* If you can't share with your grandkids what your prayers are now, you possibly can through a journal that you prepare to put into their hands someday. Nearly everyone, at some point in their life, wants to connect with their past. If you have done your job of recording your faith stories and your love for them, who knows what impact it might have on them when they finally receive them?

4. *Prepare a gift Bible for them.* I have friends who have undertaken a daunting project: creating study Bibles for their grandchildren—writing their own notes, underlining their

favorite verses, and including their own faith stories and illustrations. *You*, grandparent who is cut off from your grandchildren, can do the same for those you can't see now. When you are done, put those Bibles in a safe-deposit box if necessary, and include them in your will as gifts for your grandchildren. You never know how God might use them in a future time that you will never see.

5. *Let go of resentment toward the other grandparents* who do get to see your grandchildren. Let it *go*. Resentment won't accomplish anything good, and it will eat away at your soul.

6. *Don't give up*. Do what you can to stay in touch. If the parents will allow you to mail cards or notes, do it. Even if you suspect they are not given to the grandchild, do it. Keep them loving and gracious, and say nothing that would offend the parents.

When there is conflict with your adult child

Conflicts will almost always escalate unless someone chooses to take things in the opposite direction. If you are in conflict with your adult child, you need to take the lead in de-escalation. After all, you are the parent! Here are some thoughts about grandparent-parent conflict:

1. *Stop the war.* If you and your adult child are in a battle, it is likely that in some way, the grandchildren are the battleground. Refuse to retaliate. You will end up hurting the grandkids. Evaluate the issue in light of the potential damage to or loss of relationships in the future with your grandchildren. Is the battle really worth it? In most cases, it is not.

   Money loans, holiday plans, family traditions, or different parenting styles in areas such as discipline methods can often start the war. Be the bigger person. See the bigger picture. And refuse to sacrifice your family relationship for something more trivial.

"A person's wisdom yields patience; it is to one's glory to overlook an offense" (Proverbs 19:11).

2. *Examine your own heart* and make sure this isn't about you. Are you set on being right? Are there thoughts that make you want to justify your position? Is this an ego issue for you? If so, are you willing to make the first move in saying you are sorry for your part—even if you can't identify what that is? Here are two things you can do to help:

   a. Take time to make a sincere effort to see the conflict through your son's or daughter's eyes. How do they see you? Remember, in order to end the conflict, you will need to deal with their perception, whether it is reality or not.

   b. Pray as diligently for your attitude and your heart as you do for your adult child's. Pray Psalm 139:23–24: "Search me, God, and know my heart; test me and know my anxious thoughts. See if there is any offensive way in me, and lead me in the way everlasting."

3. *Make reconciliation the goal.* After all, that is the ministry of a believer, as we discussed in chapter 5. Reconciliation only occurs after there is repentance (that's why number 2 above is so important) and forgiveness on both sides.

Remember how patiently God waits for us sinners to repent? "The Lord is not slow in keeping his promise, as some understand slowness. Instead he is patient with you, not wanting anyone to perish, but everyone to come to repentance" (2 Peter 3:9).

Just like God does for us, you may also need to exert extreme patience—but don't ever give up doing all you can to mirror Jesus in your love, your grace, and your pursuit of reconciliation.

Managing step-grandchild relationships

Step relationships are a huge challenge, especially when the new blended family includes older children. Grandparents are often baffled about how to relate to the new family members and how to navigate the new family dynamics. Here are some things to keep in mind:

1. *Be realistic in your expectations regarding your own feelings.* When a grandchild is born into your family, you will likely feel the love and connection immediately. When the child comes in by adoption, your feelings may come more slowly. With a step-grandchild, the process is even slower yet. It is normal for you to not feel the connection right away; in fact, for some step-grand relationships, the connection will never be the same as with your natural-born grandchildren.

2. *Give them permission to take time to get to know you.* If their other grandparent relationships have been rocky or nonexistent, you may be tempted to see yourself as the grandparent-hero, riding in on a white horse to show them what a wonderful, godly grandparent is like. They may not be ready for that and may need to get to know you gradually. It's good to start off a conversation with something like this (if they are old enough): "Joey, now that our son is your new dad, we want to welcome you to our family. That means we are your step-grandparents. But don't feel pressured to call us Grandpa and Grandma. We want to get to know you and love you just like the other kids, but we know that will take time."

3. *Do everything you can to treat them the same* as your natural grandchildren. Remember that they also feel awkward, and they struggle—probably more than you—with feelings. In addition, they have also gone through some traumatic upheaval in their lives, and they need your patience

and understanding. As a *Christian* grandparent, you have a spiritual duty to love them as Jesus loves them.

Start with actions, and in time, your feelings will follow. Give them birthday and Christmas gifts equal to those you give your natural grandkids. Make an equal effort to support them in their interests, whether that means going to their school or sports events. Be willing to spend time with them equally as well—though whether that happens also should depend on their comfort level with you. You might say something like, "Joey, Grandma and I usually take Billy out for an ice cream each time we come to visit. Would you like us to do that with you as well?"

Improving relationships with your grandkids' parents

No matter what the family dynamics are, the following are simply good, sage pieces of advice that will bring improvement. We'll end with these:

1. *Let them do the parenting.* That means don't second-guess their decisions, and withhold your opinions unless they ask you what you think. Homework, discipline, eating habits, behavior standards, etc., are *their* responsibility, not yours. Remember, if there are areas that you feel need to be addressed, lean in to the relationship so that you have influence—and when they give you permission, you may share your insights with them. That means also that you should . . .

2. *Implement the parenting standards they have.* Don't undermine them. Never say, "I know your mom says _____, but . . ." You may have different standards for your home, but make sure that you communicate them in a way that still honors the parents. Don't ever sneak sweets when the parents say no, or in other ways undercut their rules. It is a guaranteed relationship-killer when the parents find out—and they will.

3. *Treat the other grandparents with respect.* You've got to do this, whether they deserve it or not. After all, speaking negatively is a surefire way to damage the relationship with your son- or daughter-in-law.

4. *Recognize the fragility of the relationship with your daughter-in-law.* This is especially for you, Grandma. You need to recognize that there is a new Mother Bear in your family. You used to be so protective of your cubs—now give her the freedom to do the same. The mother is the primary gatekeeper to the relationship with the grandchildren in most families, and putting an extra effort into building trust and love in your interactions with her will be effort well spent.

5. *Give your son-in-law a break.* After all, you likely weren't all that mature, nor did you have everything together, at his age. This is especially directed to you, Grandpa. I know you want the very best for your daughter, but do what you can to get close to her husband. The more he feels close to you and senses your love, the more he will want to be like you and listen to you.

Conclusion

I hope you've found what I promised at the beginning of the book:

- Hope—based on a new appreciation for God's principles as found in Scripture.
- Help—in the way of new strategies for approaching the hurts that are present in your family.
- Ideas—practical ones that you can begin to implement right away.

May God bring wonderful, complete healing to your hurt. May He enable you to build a spiritual legacy and leave a Jesus-shaped impression on the lives of all who follow you in your family.

NOTES

Chapter 2: Can't I Just Walk Away from the Pain?

1. Matthew 22:37
2. 1 Peter 1:15

Chapter 4: Lord, Where Is the Miracle?

1. Lewis E. Jones, "There Is Power in the Blood," 1899 on Hymnary.org, https://hymnary.org/text/would_you_be_free_from_the_burden_jones.
2. Legendary youth ministry guy, cofounder of Youth Specialties, and author of many books, including *Long-Distance Grandparenting*, which is also part of this GRANDPARENTING MATTERS series.
3. Wayne Rice, email communication with Larry Fowler.
4. Wayne Rice, email communication with Larry Fowler.

Chapter 5: The Influence Principle

1. Larry Fowler, *Raising a Modern-Day Joseph* (Colorado Springs, CO: David C. Cook, 2009), 13–14.

Chapter 6: The Grace Strategy

1. Matthew 16:23
2. Matthew 23:33
3. John 8:3–5
4. John 8:6
5. John 8:9
6. John 8:10–11
7. John 8:11

Larry Fowler is the founder of the Legacy Coalition. His vision for a national grandparenting ministry brought together a gifted team of family, children's, and youth ministry leaders to launch this movement of God. His more than forty years of ministry include experience as a youth pastor and as part of the Awana staff as a missionary, staff trainer, international director, and part of the executive leadership team. He has extensive international experience, training children's workers in forty-seven countries, and has authored five books on children's and family ministry. He is a regular main-stage speaker and workshop presenter at conferences. In 2012 he was recognized for his lifetime of contribution to children's ministry in America by the International Network of Children's Ministry with their national Legacy Award. Larry and his wife, Diane, live in Riverside, California, and have two children and seven grandchildren.

Josh Mulvihill is the executive director of church and family ministry at Renewanation, where he equips parents and grandparents to disciple their family and consults with church leaders to help them design Bible-based, Christ-centered children's, youth, and family ministries. Josh has served as a pastor for nearly twenty years, is a founding member of the Legacy Coalition, and has a PhD from the Southern Baptist Theological Seminary. He is the author of *Biblical Grandparenting*, *Preparing Children for Marriage*, and *Biblical Worldview*. Josh and his wife, Jen, live in Victoria, Minnesota, and have five children. For family discipleship resources, visit GospelShapedFamily.com.

More Grandparenting Resources

Many powerful voices are influencing our grand-children, from those at home and in their schools to those in the world of entertainment and media. Dr. Josh Mulvihill gives you all the information, insight, and ideas you need to invest spiritually in your grandkids, from sharing with unbelieving grand-children to discipling them to a mature faith. This book is perfect for individual use, with small groups, or in Sunday school classes. A DVD is also available for additional study.

Grandparenting and Grandparenting DVD

With depth and relevance, this leadership book places grandparenting ministry on a firm scriptural foundation. Ideal for pastors and church leaders, as well as for use in the classroom at seminaries, this resource is perfect for helping you show how grandparents can invest spiritually in their grandkids and speak wisdom and godliness into their lives.

Biblical Grandparenting

This brief and insightful book for church leaders offers practical guidance on how to begin a grandparenting ministry in your church. Discover tools and resources to help grandparents share their faith with and disciple a new generation.

Equipping Grandparents

✦ BETHANYHOUSE

Stay up to date on your favorite books and authors with our free e-newsletters. Sign up today at bethanyhouse.com.

facebook.com/BHPnonfiction

@bethany_house_nonfiction

@bethany_house

You May Also Like . . .

Living far away from your grandchildren is hard. But just because you can't spend as much time with them as you'd like doesn't mean you can't have an impact on their lives. In this practical book, you'll learn how to make the most of the opportunities you do have to connect with your grandkids, and more importantly, how to encourage their relationships with God.

Long-Distance Grandparenting

BETHANYHOUSE